CREATE YOUR
OWN UNIVERSE

By the same authors:

A Book of Brilliant Ideas: And How to Have Them

CREATE YOUR OWN UNIVERSE

HOW TO INVENT STORIES, CHARACTERS AND IDEAS

THE BROTHERS MCLEOD

LOM
ART

First published in Great Britain in 2017 by LOM ART, an imprint of
Michael O'Mara Books Limited
9 Lion Yard
Tremadoc Road
London SW4 7NQ

A CIP catalogue record for this book is available from the British Library.

Papers used by Michael O'Mara Books Limited are natural, recyclable products made
from wood grown in sustainable forests. The manufacturing processes conform to the
environmental regulations of the country of origin.

ISBN: 978-1-910552-49-0 in paperback print format

1 3 5 7 9 10 8 6 4 2

Cover design by Greg McLeod and Claire Cater

Designed and typeset by Design 23

Printed and bound by CPI Group (UK) Ltd, Croydon, CR0 4YY

Follow us on Twitter @OMaraBooks | #cyoucreate

www.mombooks.com

We would like to thank Gaia Banks, Hugh Barker, Lucy Fawcett, George Maudsley and our families and friends for their continued support. Also the countless people we've worked with and learned from.

Contents

Introduction

Hi, I'm Greg.

He writes.

And I'm Myles.

And he draws.

Together we are The Brothers McLeod.

That's pronounced Mac-Cloud for those of you not versed in Norse-Scottish history!

And yes, we are brothers.

We've written, drawn and made animations for lots of folks over the last few years, including Disney, DreamWorks, Aardman, the BBC and the Royal Shakespeare Company, among many others.

We've also won the occasional award for what we do, which is nice.

We like to make things. We're guessing you do too. The intention of this book is to get your brain fizzing with new ideas and to give you an idea of how to manage those ideas.

Our last book with LOM ART was *A Book of Brilliant Ideas: And How to Have Them*. That book was all about freeing yourself up and just having fun being creative.

This book is the next step. It's about how to take those ideas, how to shape them, to use that raw material to develop something coherent that you might want to share with the world.

We give you some insights into our creative process.

Plus there's a whole bunch of fun interactive exercises. Some are focused on a particular task. But some are just random and are there to help you loosen up.

There are writing exercises and illustration exercises. It doesn't matter what you label yourself as day to day – a writer, an illustrator, a candlestick maker. No one is here to categorize you or decide what you are or are not. Being creative means trying new things.

We'd love it if you would share some of your creations on social media. Just use the #cyoucreate hashtag

We hope you have fun creating your own universe.

PART ONE

* * *

THE END
AT THE
BEGINNING

The problem with finished works of art, finished TV shows or films, or finished books is that they are so ... finished. When you want to embark on your own creative endeavours it can be inspiring but also frustrating to compare your work to other people's attempts.

What is the most overused word in the history of creativity?

GENIUS!

Yes.

He's a genius.

I read all her books, she's a flipping genius.

Oh, that song is genius.

This work of art is grade-A, total, utter, unquestionable GENIUS!

AGHHHHHHHHH!

It's hard work. It's not giving up. It's ordinary people applying themselves and producing something extraordinary and wonderful. People like you.

Most, if not all of these things, are not genius.

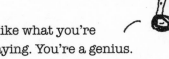

I like what you're saying. You're a genius.

Thanks. You too.

13

DRAW A MONSTER

Why?

Just do it on the page opposite, all right?

All right, touchy!

What is your monster's name? . . . .

What can they do?. . . . .

What day were they born on? . . . .

What is their weakness? . . . .

Want to share a picture of your monster on social media?
Use our #cyoumonster hashtag.

Name. Deric ..

He can shoot spikes from his tail.
birthday 31st December
Weakness. Water ...

In this book we are going to create a universe. We do this in our work as an animation company all the time. We come up with characters, locations and stories, and put them into a bible.

Not **THE** Bible, of course ...

... but **a** bible.

A creative bible contains all the things you need to know about a world that you are going to investigate through stories.

So in this book we'll help you formulate ideas that you can put into your own creative bible. We'll cover aspects of writing and drawing (because that's what we do as a pair). You can complete this book on your own, or in collaboration with someone else. You are also welcome to buy the book again (wink, wink) and fill it in with completely new ideas!

We'll start off with characters, then talk about the world and the locations and finally about creating stories. We'll also cover some other bits and bobs like gathering material from real life, creating your own language and the itch to redesign everything.

But the most important message is:

DON'T WAIT FOR PERMISSION TO BE CREATIVE

CREATE NOW!

BEGONE, INNER CRITIC! BEGONE!

Sometimes you can destroy your own creative flow before it even gets started. You have an idea and then your inner critic gets going, saying stuff like:

'Seen that before!'
'Never going to work.'
'It's a good idea, but you don't have the ability.'

Well, it's time for the critic to put a sock in it.

Draw your inner critic here. What do they look like?

Now draw a cage around your critic.

HA! HA! INNER CRITIC, YOU ARE CAGED AND CONTAINED! SO THERE.

GREG: Sometimes, when we haven't eaten enough and are having a sugar low, we think we are rubbish and fakers and shouldn't be allowed to work in the arts. We look at what other people have made and produced and think we'll never be able to achieve what they have. Because they must be GENIUSES! Then we go and have lunch and realize that we are unrecognized artists of the highest calibre and we owe it to the universe to carry on our artistic pursuits.

MYLES: Years ago, I went on a summer school run by one of the UK's best-known playwrights. Someone asked him if he ever worried that his plays weren't any good. His work is performed all over the world. He has been appointed a 'Sir' by the Queen. He has written over seventy plays. But his response was that, at the opening night of any new play, he was always worried that the audience would hate it. Like everyone else he was concerned that at any minute someone might decide he was a total fraud and had no artistic talent whatsoever.

This shows that even very successful people still worry they aren't any good. This is encouraging to the rest of us because it means our feelings of doubt are perfectly normal. This is also not encouraging, because it means we are never going to stop having these feelings!

However, if you never have any doubts about your abilities ... maybe you should. **Doubts make you question what you've created, re-evaluate, and perhaps improve!**

YOU ARE ALLOWED TO BE AN ARTIST

MYLES: What are your doubts about your abilities?
Write them down here, then look in the mirror and banish your
fears by saying the following:

'DOUBTS, YOU HAVE NO POWER OVER ME!'

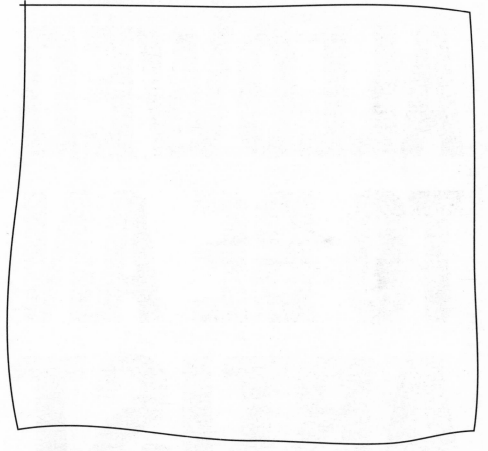

Wow. This is like therapy
or something.

The main ingredient required to finish anything is to **NOT STOP**.
The first version of something is allowed to be rubbish, or patchy,
or filled with inconsistencies. It's impossible to reshape something
you don't have. Once you have your first draft of a script, your first
sketches of characters, your first ideas for a rhyme or melody, then
you have something to work with. You have raw material. After
that, it's time to craft it into something more coherent. But there
are a million different reasons to stop.

I must first learn to
speak Spanish.

I must first order this
book and wait for it to be
delivered.

I must take up Pilates
and search for a teacher
in the local area.

I must plan my
next holiday.

I must phone that old
friend I've not spoken
to for a hundred years.

I must see if I can touch my
nose with my tongue.

RANDOMNESS MOMENT!

We've all had those spam emails dropping into our mailbox, annoying us. It's time to take the power back! Write your own spam email. Here's ours ...

'Dear Mister Buzzwidget, I am writing to you and thine friendfellows in order to sell you for the price of nothing but a tiny yet useful budgie called Desmond.'

Now you have a go!

_____

_____

_____

_____

_____

_____

_____

_____

_____

_____

_____

What are the things that stop you from finishing things?

Looking at my smartphone
too much.

What else? Write or draw these things in the space below.

MYLES: I once decided that what I needed to get myself writing a book was a grant from the Arts Council. (Not a bad idea if you need some cash to help you take time out.) But when I asked a successful author who lived near me to be my mentor, she told me I was wasting my time. What I needed to do was just sit down and write the book. I needed to stop procrastinating. She has been shortlisted for the Booker Prize, so she knows what she's talking about.

What else have you been doing to stop you from creating? Once you've written them down, strike a line through them so they no longer have any hold over you.

TV
_____

_____

_____

_____

_____

_____

_____

_____

DRAW A MONSTER

We did this already.

I know. Draw another one.
It's for a thing.

What thing?

Patience! I'll tell you
later in the book.
Just do it.

Who put you in charge?

Well, don't then.

Well, maybe I want to
draw another monster.
Ha!

What is your monster's name? . . . .

What is their greatest desire? . . . .

Do they come out in the day or night? . . . .

What is their favourite flavour

of ice cream? . . . .

**Remember, if you want to share a picture of your monster
online use our #cyoumonster hashtag.**

Name. Elphapus

Desire. Shoes . . . .
He comes out at night
ice cream choc chip mint

GREG: So, that's the end of **THE END AT THE BEGINNING.**

MYLES: Now, just put aside your doubts, your fears, silence your inner critic and create something.

GREG: And draw a picture of you smiling and happy and ready to **CREATE YOUR OWN UNIVERSE!**

PART TWO
* * *

THE
BEGINNING
AT THE
BEGINNING

In the beginning there was nothing.
Then suddenly:

BANG!

There was a bang.

And the bang felt lonely because
there were no other bangs in the universe.

But that didn't stop it worrying that it was too big a bang.
Maybe it had overdone it?

Not everything was bad, though, because suddenly there were
lots of rocks to play with and nice warm stars to sit around.

A few were yellow, which was Big Bang's favourite colour.

What are you doing?

Er ... dunno. Messing about. Telling a silly story about the Big Bang.

What? Like it was a person?

Well ... yeah.

What have I told you about messing about?

Erm ... Do more of it?

That's right. Carry on.

Ever feel like you can't have ideas? Ever feel like you have too many? Ever feel like all your ideas are worthless? Ever feel like you are an unrecognized genius? Ever feel like the idea that you really loved yesterday is a load of old crap today? Ever feel like you will never finish the thing you started? Ever feel like you are a very bad artist/writer/musician/human? Ever feel like you can't stop creating things? Yes? Welcome to the life of an artist.

Everything starts with ideas. And writers and illustrators and musicians are always being asked where their ideas come from. In most cases they haven't the faintest idea and they hate being asked this question. What worries them even more is that they might find out and in that moment will put the genie back in the bottle and never have another idea ever again. So where do ideas come from? You might be inspired by love, or death, or anger, or by another work of art. Inspiration can come when you're out walking. The science-fiction writer John Wyndham came up the germ of an idea when he was out walking in a dark country lane one night. The hedges either side of the road loomed over him and were almost indistinguishable from the night sky. He suddenly had the impression that the tall branches might flick down and sting him. Later he would go on to write *The Day of the Triffids*, the famous (and wonderful) novel featuring man-eating plants.

MYLES: Where do our ideas come from, Greg?

GREG: I get all my ideas from a mail-order company in Indianapolis. Although I'm not prepared to give you their name.

MYLES: That's a Douglas Adams quote.

GREG: Okay, okay! Hmm ... well, for some reason a lot of our stories are about communities. A lot of them are set by the sea, too.

MYLES: Oh yeah. What do you think that says about us?

GREG: It's probably the universe telling us to move to the seaside and get some friends.

Where do ideas come from?

Where do you think your ideas come from? What stories or illustrations do you like to write and draw the most?

Forget reality for a moment. Come up with one or two sentences explaining where ideas come from. Don't think about it too much. Just invent something. For example:

Ideas come from ... one-legged monkeys in the Sargasso Sea. They sing sea shanties with lyrics containing the finest thoughts known to humanity.

Ideas come from ... idea mines in the African Congo. Specialist idea miners are sent down with lamps, sketchbooks and old-fashioned tape recorders. The most famous miner was Diego Fontana Juego who mined out the entire plot of *War and Peace*, which he sold to Leo Tolstoy for three kopecks.

Ideas come from ...

Ideas come from ...

Ideas come from ...

Ideas come from ...

Our suggestions above are of the ridiculous and silly kind. Maybe that's because we create a lot of comedy-based material for animation. But your suggestions may be different. Maybe they're sad or angry or political or something else. What do your answers above say about you?

DRAW A MAN-EATING PLANT MONSTER

Time to draw another monster.
Plant-based. Man-eating, please.

Er ... we already did
two monsters.

We're making them draw
lots of monsters for something
later, all right?

Oh! Why didn't you say?

What is your monster's name? . . . .

What happens to them in autumn?. . . . .

. . . .

How do they kill their human prey? . . . .

. . . .

If they had a hobby, what would it be?. . . . .

. . . .

CREATIVE COMMUNITY

A nother really important part of coming up with ideas and developing them is community. Are you surrounded by creative people? Do you know anyone else who likes to write, draw or sing? When Shakespeare decided to make his name as a playwright, he left the tiny town of Stratford-upon-Avon and went to London. Of course, the capital offered him new opportunities to get his work in front of more people, but crucially it also exposed him to a new community. He was suddenly surrounded by a lot of creative types: other playwrights, as well as actors and minstrels. Are we suggesting you all move to London? Not unless you have a leg and arm made of gold that you are willing to sacrifice for meagre living conditions. Fortunately, we live in an age where a creative community can be found in almost every place. We're not even necessarily advocating working with those other people – it just helps to have others around you who like to be artistic. You know, instead of those people who stand over your shoulder while you're drawing something and say things like, 'Oh, you're doing a drawing. Isn't that what children do?' **Grrrrr**.

FINISH THIS DRAWING

Time for some fun. Complete this picture.

RANDOMNESS MOMENT!

It's the random moment you've all be waiting for! It's time to write the first lines of an erotic novel.

MYLES: Oh yeah! These things sell like hot buns!
GREG: Especially if they have hot buns in them.

'Peter had been secretly admiring the tight leather chinos in the shop on Blue Street for about a month now. Today, he was going to go in there and slip them on. Yes, today, Peter was going to be a new man. Peter was dead. Long live Pedro!'

GREG: That's the start of your erotic novel?
MYLES: Want to read more?
GREG: No.

Your turn!

WORKING WITH IDEAS

MYLES: What is it?

GREG: It's an idea. It just arrived.

MYLES: Looks a bit formless.

GREG: Yeah, well it's new, isn't it? We'll have to chip away at it until it reveals its inner shape.

MYLES: Like a sculpture?

GREG: Yes.

MYLES: Isn't this just a rather clumsy metaphor?

GREG: SHHH!

You may have a lot of ideas. So how do you choose which one to work on? And what happens after you pick it? There is a life cycle to ideas. Choosing ideas is just a case of listening. Usually there's one idea that nags at you more than the others.

'Me! Me! I'm a brilliant idea! Promise!'

You keep thinking about that feature film you want to write about a boat that sails back in time. You keep thinking about that little sketch of a house on spider legs. You keep thinking about that lyric for a song about a baboon wearing blue shoes. This is the idea you should probably focus on. At least today. The life cycle of ideas means that after you've worked on it a bit you might go right off it and stick it back in a drawer. There are then two courses of action:

1. Don't give up and work through the pain barrier. (This is what you have to do on commissioned projects, so it can work.)

2. Let it live in a drawer for a while and gestate until you feel the need to revisit it. (This is what you do if you're happy to grow it slowly, though – caution – you may never finish it.)

Either way, you will definitely go through several moments of creative doubt where you think the whole thing is a giant waste of time and you must be a fool for even attempting it. That's natural.

YOUR IDEAS

So, what are your ideas? Do you have things you've noticed or remembered that won't go away? A painting or sketch you did that you love and want to do more with? Or some small moments in life that you keep coming back to? Perhaps they are incidents that were very personal, but which might have broad recognition for lots of other people. Or maybe it's stuff that makes you angry that you want to talk about.

What are the ideas or stories or pictures that won't go away for you? Write about them or draw images that you associate with those ideas here and opposite, and you'll begin to have a record of your best and brightest.

My ideas that won't go away ...

CREATIVITY DOESN'T COME FROM DRUGS AND BOOZE.

CREATIVITY COMES FROM HAVING A GOOD NIGHT'S SLEEP.

COMPETITIONS AND EVENTS

Sometimes you feel creative, but aren't sure what to create. This is where competitions and social media events can come in handy.

GREG: It's nice if you win a competition, but that's just a pleasant side effect.

MYLES: The best thing about them is that they give you a set of parameters to work within.

GREG: They might be organized by genre: horror, crime or fantasy.

MYLES: Or might have a keyword to inspire you: rebellion, symbols, mercy.

GREG: They might have a target age group or, if it's a story, a number of words you must not exceed.

Events like **Inktober**, created by Jake Parker, are also fun. For the thirty-one days of October he encourages people to make one ink drawing a day. Amateurs and professionals alike share their creations using the **#inktober** hashtag. Everyone responds to the same keyword prompts. How they (and you) respond is entirely personal to you. In 2016 some of those prompts included **fast**, **rock**, **hidden**, **squeeze**, **one dozen** and **wreck**. Pick one of these prompts and make your own Inktober sketch below (even if it isn't October!)

HOW MANY IDEAS SHOULD I HAVE?

It can be frustrating when you have lots of ideas that you want to work on, but not enough time. We deal with this by doing little bits of work on an idea and then filing them away – so we capture that initial burning enthusiasm, try to encourage the idea to form into something useful, and then park it until we have time to work on it some more. This often happens with our short films. They may start as little tiny animations, or a synopsis for a story.

Now you may be wondering how many ideas it's normal to have in one day, week or month. Who knows? It's different for everyone. It is likely that your creative community will contain at least one zealous individual who has had only one idea and has religiously tried to realize it over a thirty-year period without success. They will tell you about this idea in great depth, whether you would like to hear about it or not. This will be made worse by the fact that this type of individual always seems to have diabolical halitosis. This person is to be avoided if you value your sanity. If you are this person, please try to have another idea.

'Have I shown you my amazing idea for an educational series for children based on paperclips and shoehorns? It's called *Clippy Hornface and the Pencil Friends*.'
'AGHHHHH!'

Probably the worst thing you can do is not do anything. You don't get better by not starting. Just have a go. Sometimes you'll create a thing of beauty. Sometimes you'll create a monstrous load of old crap. That's fine. Just keep going. And when you have some time and distance, go back and look at that disaster to try to work out why it didn't succeed. Stand-up comedians are well known for recording their own shows so they can listen back to them to see which bits worked well, and which bits bombed. Then they rework their show over and over until it's honed and slick.

Occasionally you may just feel like you are totally empty of creativity and ideas. You may think it's time to abandon your creative urges. This is also a very familiar stage. You may think that attempting to force yourself to be creative is the correct response. It probably isn't. If you are feeling empty then it's time to fill up on life experiences again – then you'll have something to respond to. So, possible cures for this condition include:

- **Sleep**
- **Stop giving in to self-pity**
- **Read**
- **Travel**
- **See friends**

What are the things you like to do? What helps you recharge? What inspires you? Draw or write those things here:

_____

_____

_____

_____

_____

Draw to music

Sometimes it's fun to create something for no particular reason.
It can help you to loosen up and just enjoy the moment. Play some
jazz. Listen to it. Pay attention to how it makes you feel.
Then begin to draw below.

In this section we've concentrated on ideas. Where ideas come from is both obvious and also a huge mystery. They come from living our lives. But they also feel like they pop out of the ether into our heads like little messages from who knows where. The key thing is to listen to them, capture them, note them down and then later you can decide which ones you would like to develop into something more. In the next part, we'll look at creating characters, then worlds, then stories!

So is this the end of the beginning at the beginning?

Yes, the beginning of the beginning is now at an end.

PART THREE
***

CHARACTERS

GREG: Creating characters is like cleaning.

MYLES: You're never sure where to start and you'll never be finished.

GREG: There's no right or wrong way to start creating characters.

MYLES: A character might be a facsimile of somebody you know.

GREG: They might represent a part of your own personality.

MYLES: A character might be based on someone interesting from a news story, or from history.

GREG: They might just have popped into your head from who knows where.

MYLES: A character might begin with a sketch, a sound, a quote. A piece of music, even.

GREG: Whoever they are, this character will evolve the more you get to know them – the more you write about them, the more you draw them, the more you think about them.

Characters don't exist in isolation, of course. Most books, TV shows, films and graphic novels have a single character at the heart of their story. Yes, sometimes it's about two main characters who orbit around each other as 'buddies', but most of the time you'll have one key character at the heart of your world. The identity of this character will affect all the other characters you create. In a way, everyone else exists to complement, help, tempt, or antagonize this character. If your main character is the sun, then the other characters are planets in orbit around him or her.

MYLES: A famous British playwright once told me that he created characters based on people he knew, and to hide their real identity he would change their gender. Usually the person had no idea they had been the basis for one of his characters. Usually.

Write a character description of someone interesting that you know.
Disguise them as an imaginary character. You could draw them on the
next page, too.

_____

_____

_____

_____

_____

_____

_____

_____

_____

_____

_____

_____

_____

_____

Draw them!

PERSONAL MONSTER

So you just created a character based on someone you know ... now imagine that they had a personal monster that liked to hang around with them. It could be a smart monster that's a buddy or a partner, or a pet-like monster that they own, or perhaps a daemon that they must always remain close to.

What is your monster's name? . . . .

How are they similar or different to their human? . . . .

. . . .

How many toes do they have? . . . .

Can they breathe fire? If so, what colour is the fire? . . . . . .

Now draw it!

GREG: Hey we've got a whole bunch of monster characters going on.

MYLES: Rarg bethorl noogaf gruntee munt.

GREG: Huh?

MYLES: That's monsterish for, 'I know. It's great, isn't it?'

GREG: You need to get out more.

BEARDS AND HAIR

Time for some nonsense! Add hair to these characters to bring out their personality.

PROFESSOR LUNARBOX

MAJOR NASTYMAN

MISS DWARVENFORGE

JEMIMA SPLENDID

GEORGIE SQUINTFACE

JUDGE KNOCKERDOWN

JUST**CREATE**

When you're first populating a world with characters it's best not to worry about whether you'll use them or not. Just have fun creating. The best or most useful ones will emerge naturally. Sometimes it can be helpful to visualize the characters – you can do this by drawing them, or by grabbing pictures of actors you think would be good to play the part.

At some point you'll have to stop focusing on who these characters are and start to think about how these characters interact with each other. Which characters are friends? Which ones are related? Who hates who? Why? Who is being two-faced? Who is hiding something from the others? When you start mapping this out in your head – or on the page – the characters start to create a fabric, a world around them. You may start having ideas for stories based on their relationships. You may start to think about where they live in relation to each other.

Here are some characters ...

Now draw your own on the next page. Just do it. Off the top of your head. Don't think about it too much. Just let your pen wander. Remember, this book isn't about whether you're a writer, a poet, an illustrator, a musician or a plumber. It's about letting the ideas flow. Just have a go and see what you create.

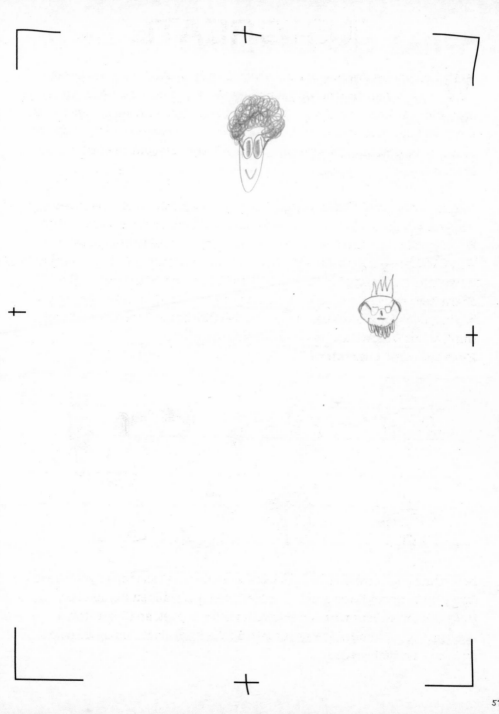

WHAT COMES FIRST?

When you're creating a universe, it's not always the characters that come first. Perhaps it's a particular story, or a place? There's no right or wrong way.

Let's say you're creating a character to go with a **story idea** you've had. The story is about a person who accidentally summons a demon.

Who is the person? How do they respond to the demon? What does the demon want?

_____

_____

_____

_____

_____

_____

_____

_____

_____

_____

_____

Let's say you're creating a character because you've been inspired by the idea of a particular **PLACE**.

You want to write a story set in a secret valley between tall mountains. Who finds this place? Who lives there? What are they doing there? What do they want?

_____

_____

_____

_____

_____

_____

_____

_____

_____

_____

_____

_____

_____

_____

INTERNAL AND EXTERNAL WORLDS

How can characters differ in books versus films? Well, for a start, in books and graphic novels we are often privy to the internal thoughts of the characters. We know what they are thinking. This only happens in films if there's some kind of voice-over and that can often be clunky. Characters in written works can let us into their inner world a lot more easily.

In films we respond to characters based on a more external view of them. Rather than having the advantage of seeing their inner life, we have to understand their desires through their physical actions alone.

BOB AND HELEN - GRAPHIC NOVEL

BOB AND HELEN - FILM STORYBOARD

Oh, sorry, Helen. I had no idea you were here.

Think about a character you like from a particular film. Why did you like them? How did you know who they really were? What did they really stand for? Was it how they looked, or what they said, or was it what they did?

CHARACTER
IS
ACTION

YES, CHARACTER **IS** ACTION

Characters say all kinds of things, but it's what they do (or don't do) that really counts.

GREG: Hey, Myles, what about some examples of how character is action?

MYLES: Good idea, Greg!

In Shakespeare's play, *Richard III*, in Act 3 Scene 7, Richard complains that he doesn't want to be king. He says to those pleading for him to take the crown, 'Alas, why would you heap these cares on me? I am unfit for state and majesty; I do beseech you, take it not amiss; I cannot nor I will not yield to you.' What he says is very clear. He does not want to be king. But we know from his actions (murdering his brother, killing off his nephews) that this is exactly what he wants. He is pretending to be humble to help persuade others that he is just the kind of monarch they need. Richard's actions reveal his true self: a despotic, homicidal villain.

In *Star Wars: Episode IV – A New Hope*, smuggler Han Solo is stacking up his reward money and leaving his friends before the big fight at the end. His defence for not helping is, 'What good's a reward if you ain't around to use it?' It seems like he's a typical small-time criminal taking the easy way out. But then, at the crucial moment in the final battle, he risks his life, flies in and clears a path for Luke Skywalker to destroy the Death Star. Han's actions reveal his true self: a friend and a hero.

YOUR FOUR PANELS

Draw a four-panel comic where we are privy to the internal thoughts of the character. Perhaps have the same pose in each panel – so no action at all if you want.

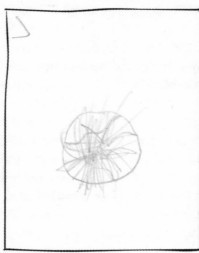

Now draw a four-panel comic where we are unaware of the internal thoughts of the character. How can you demonstrate what they want by action alone? How can you contrast it with what they say?

CHARACTER QUESTIONS

Sometimes you create a character and have a good feel for who they are. You need to bring that feeling into focus. Character questionnaires can help you crystallize those feelings.

Come up with some characters without thinking about the answers too much. Just try to respond quickly and instinctively. Who will you create?

FIRST NAME: _Tig_

SURNAME: _Belles_

**SECRET MIDDLE NAME
THEY TELL NO ONE ABOUT:** _Bond_

HOMETOWN: _Trevagen_

FAVOURITE INSECT: _lady bug_

FAVOURITE PUDDING: _Apple crumble_

FAVOURITE COLOUR: _Mint_

POLITICAL VIEWS: _Green party_

**IF THEY WERE A PLANET, WHICH
ONE WOULD THEY BE?** _Earth_

**WHERE WOULD THEY HAVE A
SECRET HIDEOUT?** _on a cloud_

Let's go again ...
but with different
answers.

FIRST NAME: _Bubble_

SURNAME: _PoP_

**SECRET MIDDLE NAME
THEY TELL NO ONE ABOUT:** _Water_

HOMETOWN: _Michaelstow_

FAVOURITE INSECT: _shield bug_

FAVOURITE PUDDING: _Apple pie_

FAVOURITE COLOUR: _Green_

POLITICAL VIEWS: _Blue Party_

**IF THEY WERE A PLANET, WHICH
ONE WOULD THEY BE?** _Mars_

**WHERE WOULD THEY HAVE A
SECRET HIDEOUT?** _under ground_

CHARACTER QUESTIONS

Make up your own character questions here. They can be straightforward, like 'When were they born?' or more metaphorical like 'What animal would they be?' or they can be fun and silly: 'If they had to wear a cake on their head, what kind of cake would that be?' It's really just about getting to know your characters better. Once you've written your questions, why don't you ask a friend to answer them. See what they come up with. Does it inspire you?

HOW DO WE CREATE CHARACTERS?

MYLES: So, Greg, how do you create a character?

GREG: If there's a script I read it and get a sense of who the
characters are. Then I draw something that I feel fits
the character. I try to capture the physicality of that
character. If there's no script, I often just design the
characters straight out of my head. I just go with the flow of
consciousness and see what happens.

Myles, how do you create a character?

MYLES: Often I'll have an idea for a story and an instinct for the
character who's going to go on that journey. I suppose most
of my characters are a little bit like me in some way. I can't
tell you how many stories I've come up with about reticent,
introverted characters who battle against their shyness
and fear of failure in order to succeed.

GREG: Are you still shy?

MYLES: Shhh! I'm hiding.

WHO ARE YOU CREATING FOR?

Who are you creating your characters for?
Yourself? A client? No one?

GREG: A few years ago we came up with a
story for my son about a knight.
MYLES: So we wrote and illustrated it to
appeal to an audience of one.
GREG: Just my son.
MYLES: And, in a strange way, that made it
easier to create. We just focused on
him and what he liked and what made him laugh.
GREG: He loved it.

If you were going to write a story for one person, who would that
be and what would the story be?

_____

_____

_____

_____

_____

_____

_____

_____

_____

CREATING TO ORDER

GREG: At some point someone may ask for your help in creating a fictional world.

MYLES: We've done this for a variety of folks, including Aardman, the BBC, the Royal Shakespeare Company and DreamWorks.

GREG: Are you showing off again?

MYLES: Just stating facts.

GREG: Well okay then ... and, by the way, you forgot Disney.

MYLES: When you're creating characters for a client, then you might have to do some research. When I developed the new version of Noddy, the only real stipulation was that he had to be a detective. Most other aspects were up for grabs. My job was to help create a fresh TV show for kids that was faithful to the original Noddy stories, while being more relevant to a twenty-first century audience. I looked back at the original books and thought to myself: these toys are what you could buy in the shops when this book came out. But you can't get them now. In other words, if Enid Blyton had written Noddy now, which toys might she have included in her books?

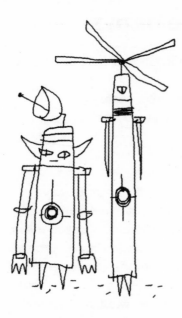

Of course, we kept some classic characters. There's still Noddy's car, Bumpy Dog and Big Ears. But there are new toys too: a dinosaur with her own science lab, an up-to-the-minute robot (I'd seen too many retro robots in preschool shows) and some lovable pandas (mainly because I remembered how much my sister had loved them as a little girl). There is also a superhero action toy called ...

GREG: Deltoid! I know that ... because I came up with his name. Fact!

MYLES: Not all of my ideas were used, and some of the characters were modified through the creative to and fro between executives, directors, producers and so on. But my job was to come up with a lot of ideas and throw them into the mix. It was to get things started!

Imagine you've been asked to reimagine a classic story for children – perhaps a folk tale, a biblical story like Noah's Ark, or a more recent classic like *Peter Pan* or *The Wind in the Willows*. Now imagine you have to set the story in modern times. What kind of characters would you keep from the original, how would you make them relevant to a modern audience, and would you create any new characters? Draw the characters and write short biographies on the opposite page:

SILHOUETTES

Can you identify a character just by their silhouette? Think of Mickey Mouse, SpongeBob SquarePants, Totoro. They all have unique silhouettes that make them immediately identifiable. Try making your own strong character silhouettes here. Have a play.

With a cast of characters you might want them to all have the same silhouette. See how different you can make these characters with the same silhouette.

You might also want your characters to have totally different silhouettes, like these ones. Try making your own.

CHARACTER NAMES

A character doesn't begin to come alive until you have named them. It's like a magic spell: if you know your character's true name you will start to be able to control them.

GREG: Do you find it hard to come up with character names? Or do you just hit it?

MYLES: I often come up with the names of characters quite quickly. But I'll also trust my instinct. If I've named a character but I'm not sure about it, I'll search out other names.

GREG: There are lots of baby-naming websites on the internet that are useful.

MYLES: But also watch out for funny or interesting real names that you can use or adapt.

GREG: Here are some great names we've collected from spam emails and other moments:

 Stirling Ward

 John Cold

 Romeo Calhoun

 Carol Cobelfret

 Richard Ladymonks

 Jolly Bunting

 Trenton Williamson

Search through your emails for some ridiculous and splendid names and mix and match them.

Come up with your own names here.

Name: _Tolly Longy_

Name: _Elman Sigsam_

Name: _____

Name: _____

Name: _____

Name: _____

Name: _____

Name: _____

Name: _____

Name: _____

Now draw them.

Does their name create an image of a type of person?

THINK OF A NUMBER BETWEEN ONE AND ONE HUNDRED.

Write the number here.

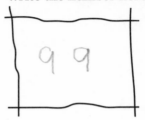

Imagine this number had a personality. What would that be?

_____

_____

_____

_____

_____

_____

_____

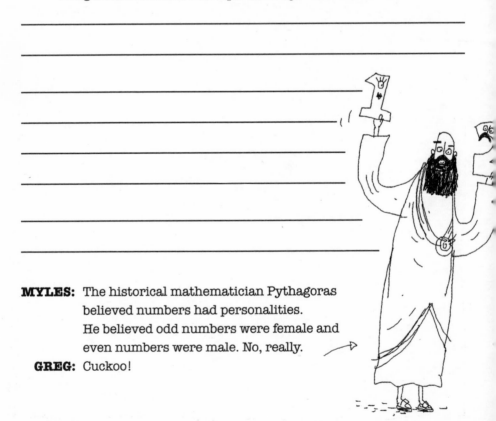

MYLES: The historical mathematician Pythagoras
believed numbers had personalities.
He believed odd numbers were female and
even numbers were male. No, really.

GREG: Cuckoo!

**Draw your favourite number, but as a character,
showing his or her unique personality.**

First Memory

What's the first thing you remember?
Why do you think this memory has stayed with you?

FINISH THIS DRAWING

Complete this picture. Don't think about it too much;
just do what feels instinctive.

FLAWLESS CHARACTERS

We've written and produced animation for children's TV. There's often a pressure to make characters that have very positive outlooks on life, especially for preschool shows. This makes sense, of course – we don't want TV to scare three-year-olds. We want them to have positive role models and not learn bad behaviours from their favourite programmes. But this effort to make characters positive can sometimes make them unrealistic.

A character who is not worried by anything, who can do anything easily, who doesn't get upset, or who doesn't upset anyone else is fairly useless in creative terms. If nothing ever bothers them then where is the drama? Where is the character's journey? BORING!

The worst thing about characters like this is that they are lies. No one is perfect. No one is okay all the time. No one is flawless. Pretending some people are perfect means you're not being truthful.

The people who love us most – the ones who know us best – know our flaws. They know what makes us feel vulnerable. And we know their flaws, too. We forgive each other for them; we help each other deal with them. It's what makes us care about each other and therefore is what makes us care about well-conceived characters – we latch on to the realism on show.

Think of yourself, your friends and family. And think of those people who rub you up the wrong way. What are their flaws? Write them here.

_____

_____

_____

_____

_____

_____

_____

_____

_____

_____

_____

_____

_____

_____

_____

Can you use these flaws when you're creating your own characters?

FEMALE CHARACTERS

A quick note about female characters. If your female characters are only defined in relation to the male characters, for example, or if you only define them by which man they are in love with ... you need to enter the twenty-first century.

Psst! Check out the Bechdel test.

RANDOMNESS MOMENT!

And now the exciting new novel by YOU entitled ...

CONFESSIONS OF A WEREWOLF WITH A BOAT FIXATION

CHAPTER ONE:
The Wereboat

You take over now. Write something here and don't stop until you reach the end of the next double-page spread. Don't think too much about what you're writing. It can be as nonsensical as you like. Just let the pencil or pen keep going.

This is a free- or auto-writing exercise. The key thing is to start and not stop and let your train of thought take you wherever. Sometimes you can create crazy new ideas this way. Sometimes it's just gobbledegook.

CONFESSIONS OF A WEREWOLF WITH A BOAT FIXATION

The Wereboat

HISTORICAL AND INSPIRATIONAL

Where else can you get inspiration for characters? Well, what about historical people of interest, or inspiring people out there in the world today? You might want to create something about that person, or just use them as the basis for a new creation.

Who do you find inspiring, Greg?

Pablo Picasso.　　**Man Ray.**　**Nick Cave.**　**David Bowie.**

What about you, Myles?

Sir Joseph Banks was an interesting chap. Inherited a pile of money and could have just sat back, lazed around and lived the high life. Instead he pursued a career as a pioneering botanist. He booked himself on to a potentially life-threatening trip around the world with Captain Cook. He came back with samples of hundreds of plants previously unknown to science. Wow! What a guy!

What about you? Who inspires you?
Can you use this person in your universe? Can you disguise them as a character?

BUBBLES OF AMBITION

Draw yourself at the centre of these bubbles. What are your ambitions? Not just creative ambitions, but any type of ambition. Write them into the bubbles.

Do your ambitions relate to the kinds of stories you want to write, or the things you like to read and watch?

SECRET TRUTHS

Do you wonder what people are holding back? What their secrets are? What they truly desire but cannot say? This is what lies behind the popularity of the **'PostSecret'** phenomenon that's been running for a few years now.

Have a look for the books, or the blog. You'll find the anonymous postcards with their fascinating messages. Many of them are quite sad and upsetting cries for help, revealing the inner turmoil of our fellow humans. Some are naughty or cheeky – for example, there's one that reads: 'I get jealous of people who can solve Rubik's Cubes. (So I switch the stickers and watch them struggle!)'

If you were to send them an anonymous postcard, what would you reveal? You might not want to write that in this book, of course. Buy a postcard. Send it to **PostSecret**. What are you hiding inside? What is your secret?

SHOES

Time for some silliness! Shoes can say a lot about a person. Add shoes to these characters to bring out their

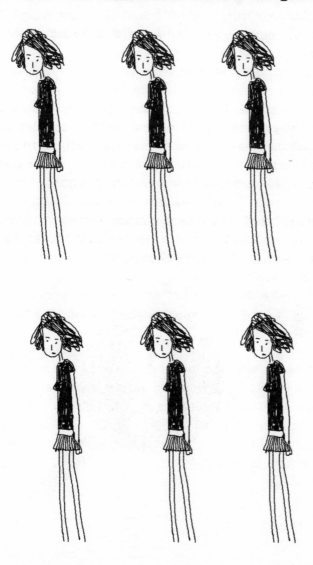

BORROWING

GREG: When you say borrowing, you mean ... stealing?

MYLES: Well ... stealing, borrowing ... what's the difference?

GREG: That's a relief, because I 'borrowed' your lunch.

MYLES: I once went to hear a renowned TV writer talk about his work. During questions and answers I asked him how he came up with the characters in his most successful show. He said he'd stolen them from a 1980s film that he loved. There was an athlete, a nerdy brainbox, a rebel, a princess and a criminal in that film. That's what appeared in his TV show, too. They weren't exactly the same and the context was completely different, but it worked, so you could say it was stealing with affection to create something new.

It's fine to be inspired by someone else's creation and to find a way of using it in your own work. Just don't copy it exactly. Be inspired by it.

When we were kids we used to watch loads of old 1920s and 30s Laurel and Hardy films on our dad's reel-to-reel. We also loved watching the 1940s and 50s Chip 'n' Dale cartoons. Ever noticed how similar Chip is to Hardy and Dale is to Laurel? We're not saying anyone stole anything, but the relationship dynamic is similar.

RANDOMNESS MOMENT!

Draw a character with two heads. They wear an interesting Christmas jumper. GO!

example

CASTS OF CHARACTERS

So let's say you have a character you want to work with. Trying to work out who the other characters in this universe are can be tricky. When you get stuck, here are a few ideas to think about.

'Powers'

Characters have a world view, a mindset. The story consultant Laurie Hutzler identifies nine 'powers' behind characters. They are Reason, Truth, Will, Ambition, Idealism, Imagination, Love, Conscience and Excitement. A power can have both a light and a dark side to it: **AMBITION** can drive a sportswoman to win a gold medal through hard work, or it can drive a prince to kill off his rivals so he can become king.

Characters may have more than one power, but usually there will be one that dominates the rest. Do they have an incurable desire to uncover the **TRUTH** like Sherlock Holmes? Or are they relentlessly looking for **EXCITEMENT** like Iron Man? Do they have a relentless **WILL** to control events like Michael Corleone in the *Godfather* films?

How does having a cast of characters with different motivations create interesting conflicts and allegiances?

When you next watch an episode of your favourite TV show, or watch a film, try to identify which powers the different characters express the most. Write down your findings here.

You can read a lot more about character powers on Laurie Hutzler's website. Get thee to a search engine!

HEAD, HEART, FEET

Another way to look at characters is **head, heart, feet**.

MYLES: I've been fortunate enough to work with some wonderful script editors. They've helped make my scripts better by working with me on character shortcomings, plot inconsistencies and clarity, clarity, clarity. One of these is Hannah Rodger. She related a wonderful pearl of wisdom from her father, Roy. He'd noticed that most stories seemed to have three characters that could be described as head, heart and feet.

 The head is a thinker, someone that relies on their brains to interact with the universe around them.

 The heart uses love and empathy (or even hate) to deal with the world. They respond with their emotional instincts.

 The feet is a doing character; someone who runs into the action full tilt without thinking.

Just as before, see if you can spot them in the next book you read, or TV show or film you watch. What did you conclude?

THE FOUR TEMPERAMENTS

There have been all kinds of theories for the differences in human personality over the centuries. One from early Greek medicine is the idea of the four humours. The Greeks had this great notion that the different balance of bodily fluids affected people's health and behaviours. The four humours were blood, yellow bile, black bile and phlegm, and were aligned with the four elements air, water, earth and fire. Each manifested a different temperament:

Sanguine (blood)
Lively, friendly, optimistic. They are associated with Air, and with the Spring season

Choleric (yellow bile)
Impatient, irritable, impulsive.
Associated with Fire and the Summer

Melancholic (black bile)
Serious, practical, quiet. Associated with Earth and Autumn

Phlegmatic (phlegm)
Benevolent, thoughtful, empathetic.
Associated with Water and Winter

Draw four faces that you feel match these characteristics on the next page.

If you put the four people from the previous page into a room together to talk about rising house prices, how would that conversation go? What would be their different outlooks?

_____

_____

_____

_____

_____

_____

_____

_____

_____

_____

_____

_____

_____

_____

COMEDY CHARACTERS

If you're struggling to create a cast of characters, then study some of your favourite plays, books, films and TV shows, and see how they made a success of it. That's right. STEAL! But don't copy. You're just stealing the inspiration!

Now think of some of your favourite sitcoms or comedies. What are the main defining features of each character? They will all be seriously flawed in some way, but in what way?

Are they neurotic or uptight?

Perhaps they are stupid?

Or really offbeat or leftfield with their own logic?

Are they a voracious predator of the opposite sex?

Are they lovable like a puppy but also weak or cowardly?

Are they really smart, but also cynical?

Are they just a real bastard?

Are they very materialistic?

COMMEDIA

The commedia dell'arte is a form of comedy from Italy with a long history. They used archetypal characters that are still identifiable in modern sitcoms. There's a real hierarchy for these characters with leaders, masters, servants and peasants. Hierarchies are great for drama and comedy. Who's trying to climb the greasy pole, or impress their master, or fool their boss, and which leader is trying to swindle his own servants or employees? Check out the National Theatre's YouTube videos about this kind of theatre; they're really insightful.

Magnifico

He's the leader of the city. The most powerful person.

Pantalone

A master. He's a merchant and a miserly old man. He doesn't have Magnifico's power. He's a vinegary sort of person with a lot of needs. What a meany.

Doctor

Another master, the Doctor professes to be a man of learning who knows everything about everything, but understands nothing. He can waffle on for ages. What a windbag.

Columbina

She has aspects of the masters and servants. She's cunning, playful, knowledgeable and thrifty.

Brighella

He's the master of servants and the servant of masters. He's cunning. He can be a womanizer, too.

Arlecchino

Another servant. He's cheeky and not as smart as Brighella. He's very physical, and thinks he's gorgeous. Arlecchino lives in the moment.

Il Capitano

Il Capitano is a braggart and a coward. He's a mercenary soldier who always avoids the fight.

Zanni

At the bottom of the pecking order, the Zanni or Zannis represent the workers, usually peasants from the countryside. They are crazy, curious and enthusiastic. (Note that Arlecchino and Brighella are specialized forms of Zanni).

Why not draw your own versions of these characters
from these short descriptions?

Draw to music

Play some Christmas songs. Listen to them. Pay attention to how they make you feel. Then begin to draw below.

GO TO THE
CHARITY SHOP AND
BUY AN OUTFIT

+

WEAR IT AND
WALK AROUND

+

HOW DO YOU
FEEL?

+

WHO ARE YOU?

MASKS

Traditional theatre like commedia uses masks to help externalize a character's personality. They have distinctive noses and brows. Similarly, Japanese Kabuki theatre uses elaborate make-up for different characters. Add detail to these masks below to help reveal their character.

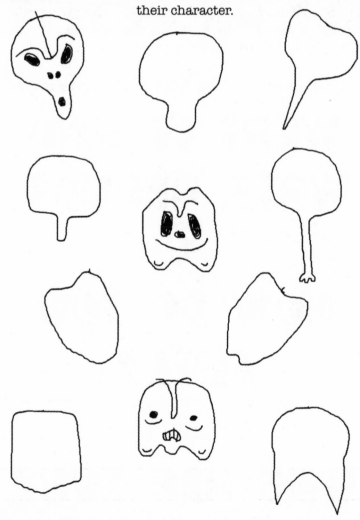

Families

A lot of stories are about families. There are so many relationship dynamics to play with. One family might have a mother who writes novels by night, a father with a drinking habit, rebellious twins and an adopted child with the power to move things with her mind. Another family might have a mother who's a soldier on tour with the army, a father who is secretly in love with his best friend and a son with a fascination for lizards.

WRITE OUT IDEAS FOR YOUR OWN FAMILY HERE

Family Dynamics

It can be useful to think of the family dynamic when creating a cast of characters. Lots of shows have a metaphorical family. They use the dynamics between family members as the dynamics between friends, or work colleagues. The writer Graham Linehan describes how his comedy series *Father Ted* (created with Arthur Mathews) about three priests features separate characters who together form a kind of family: Father Ted, young Father Dougal, old Father Jack and housekeeper Mrs Doyle.

Why don't you try creating a group of work colleagues who have a family dynamic? Remember they're not related by blood, but there is a mother figure, a father figure, a grandfatherly character and so on.

MYLES: A true family may have stronger bonds, of course, so you may be able to pull them further apart in the drama and still have them snap back together again. Just think of all the horrible things Homer does in *The Simpsons*. But he and Marge always kiss and make up at the end. Having said that, not all families are that close.

GREG: Yeah, you wouldn't believe the amount of times people ask us how often we fall out.

MYLES: Says more about their family relationships, I think.

GREG: Ouch!

POLITE SNOOPING

What do your characters sound like? How do they sound different? We don't just mean their accents; we mean the manner of their speech. Is it precise or lazy? Are they staccato or do they talk in a kind of rhythm? Do they rarely speak? Are they a chatterbox?

Try sitting in a cafe or bar or near someone on a park bench. Take out your notebook and look busy ... but snoop on what those around you are saying. Write it down. Sketch them, too, if you like. A lot of what they say will be banal, but sometimes you'll hear something very interesting. What did they say? What does it reveal?

CONSISTENCY

Hopefully you now have a few ideas for characters and their traits. We've encouraged you to be free with your creativity. The first stage of creating should not even involve criticizing what you are making. Just create. Of course, once you start to develop a character, you may want to start thinking more critically.

Once your character starts coming alive you need to keep an eye on his or her consistency. Don't make them do something because it's convenient for your story; the character must always be consistent with the personality you have created. That doesn't mean you can't put them under pressure, or see them break down or act in an unusual way. It just has to be logical.

In fact, making it more difficult and less convenient for your characters will lead to a more interesting and more satisfying story!

OPPOSITES

A key idea in drama is opposition: a character has an intention and there are obstacles in the way. The obstacles can be things in the environment (like weather, mountains or a wall), things in their own mind (like doubts or fears) or other people. Take a look at one of the characters you've created. Now create their exact opposite. Think about it – this is the basis of so many stories. How many times have you heard this kind of thing in a film?

GOODY: At last, villain of this story, I have cornered you and you will be punished in some way!

BADDY: *Stop, hero! Think about it … you and I are just the same.*

GOODY: No, we aren't!

BADDY: *Yes, we are. We both have the same interests and do similar things!*

GOODY: That's not true.

BADDY: *Yes it is!*

GOODY: Well, okay, it is a bit, but I do those things in a nice way and you do them in a nasty way.

BADDY: *That's not true.*

GOODY: Yes it is!

BADDY: *Okay. So we're the same, but kind of different. What is that?*

GOODY: We're opposites, you dufus.

BADDY: *Oh, yes. I suppose we are. But there's one more thing …*

GOODY: Yes?

BADDY: *I AM YOUR FATHER!*

This happens because it's the basis of a lot of stories. A character confronts his or her opposite. They are changed by the encounter, perhaps absorbing some of the qualities of their opposite to become more complete and balanced.

Seen the Marvel film *Thor*? (If not, spoiler alert!) He is a powerful warrior with a big ego. Then he's cast out of Asgard without his hammer and learns humility. In the end he regains his power, but now wields it with wisdom.

What about the children's book *Room on the Broom*? (Spoiler alert again.) The witch is unfailingly generous, giving seats away on her broom. But her generosity results in the broom breaking and everyone falling into a muddy bog. After a near fatal encounter with a dragon, they create a new broom with places for each of the passengers (including a shower for the frog, which is a brilliant idea).

If you're wondering what we're on about, go and look up the terms thesis, antithesis and synthesis for more.

MYLES: As a child I used to love the children's book *Fattypuffs and Thinifers* by André Maurois. It was a simple story of some fat people at war with some thin people and how they sorted out their differences. It worked so well on a visual level because they were literal opposites.

Use these shapes to draw your character opposites here.

ANTAGONISTS

Talking of opposites, most stories revolve around a single character. This person is the protagonist. This is derived from fancy Greek words: **protos**, meaning 'first in importance', and **agonistes**, meaning 'actor'. The protagonist's opposite is termed the antagonist.

GREG: You know, it's God versus the Devil.

MYLES: It's cop versus robber.

GREG: It's human versus alien.

MYLES: It's cat versus dog.

GREG: It's Nigel Thrumpwidget versus the Speckled Newt of Doom.

MYLES: Oh yeah. That's a classic.

But there doesn't have to be just one antagonist. They don't even have to be a person. The forces of antagonism can come from three places:

- A classical antagonist. Someone with desires and needs that conflict with the protagonist
- Inside the protagonist. Their own fears and doubts
- The universe. The environment around the protagonist can throw up obstacles. A mountain can be an antagonist if it's in between your home and where you want to be

But when antagonists are other people, they don't have to be 'bad guys'. They don't have to be Darth Vader or an Evil Queen with a bad apple. Hayao Miyazaki's films have some wonderful antagonists who aren't cardboard cut-out evil dudes: they are just other people with different points of view. It makes for a much richer and more interesting story sometimes.

Take his film *Princess Mononoke*. Lady Eboshi is responsible for destroying much of the beautiful forest. But at the same time she is a noble, likeable person. She looks after lepers and has helped former prostitutes find other work in her factory.

And *Ponyo*. Ponyo is a little fish who wants to be a girl. Her father tries hard to stop her ambitions, not because he is evil, but because he is disenchanted with humanity (and for good reason).

When you're creating your antagonists, think how to make them more interesting and more believable.

SWITCHERS

Some characters aren't quite what they seem to be. They appear weak, but are strong. Or appear good, but are evil. Or appear foolish, but reveal they are in fact very wise (like Yoda in *The Empire Strikes Back*). These characters seem to switch, but are in fact just hiding their true selves behind a protective mask. Why don't you create a character below – draw them here, and write a short biography on the opposite page. They could be a hero, a villain, a detective, a jester, a professor. Once you've created their true personality, decide on their mask or persona. How do they choose to appear to everyone else? And why?

The **RE**DESIGN

MYLES: Sometimes when we're well into development of an idea Greg will come to me and say ...

GREG: Hey, Myles, you know all those characters I drew?

MYLES: Yeah?

GREG: Here they are again, but in a completely different style. I just wasn't sure it was working the other way.

A while back we made a comedy pilot called *Isle of Spagg*. One character looked like this:

But halfway through development, Greg did this:

We decided we really liked the new look, but for something aimed at a younger audience than we were creating for. So we stuck with the original designs.

Why don't you draw your own version of this character opposite and see what you come up with? (You could also try creating some friends for him. Who are they? What do they want out of life?)

This kind of process of experimenting, using your doubts to find new styles, and then re-evaluating what's right for any given project, is not only normal but healthy! It also often leads to new styles we can use in other projects.

SO IN CONCLUSION...

GREG: We hope we've given you some ideas about characters, and how to create them.

MYLES: The key thing is to find inspiration from the world around you, from your own personality, and to make rounded characters with talents and flaws.

GREG: And to make them visually distinctive and, if you have a group of characters, to make each of them unique.

MYLES: Have a look back through the characters you've drawn or written about here.

GREG: Are there any that you really like, or think you could do more with? Perhaps one is the seed of a new project?

PART FOUR
* * *
WORLDS

As the creator of your universe you get to make it any kind of place you like. But let's say you have a character in mind. Can they exist just anywhere? What kind of a universe suits them?

The type of world you create should flow out of your character in some way. Would the story of Macbeth be quite so powerful and full of dread if he was living in sunny Spain?

GREG: Could be a good start to a comedy version, though!

In *Star Wars*, Luke Skywalker grows up on Tatooine, which he describes in this way: 'If there's a bright centre to the universe, you're on the planet that it's farthest from.' The place reflects his character's disenfranchisement. It's the same for Adrian Mole. In *The Secret Diary of Adrian Mole, Aged 13¾*, we find the frustrated teenage poet living in a dour corner of the Midlands in England.

But sometimes an opposite of what you expect is just what is needed.

In Stella Gibbons' novel *Cold Comfort Farm*, the place and the protagonist Flora Poste are opposites. She is relentless in her pursuit of positivity, but the farm is a place of cold comforts indeed. How will the character affect the world and vice versa?

When you're creating worlds, think about your main character and how they might exist in a world that either reflects or opposes their personality.

'**When shall we three meet again?**'

'**In thunder, lightning or in rain?**'

'**What about in the pool?**'

Maps

Let's create our first world! Who doesn't love drawing maps of imaginary places?

Draw an island here. Mark places of interest. Give your island a name.

MYLES: I don't know about you, but just drawing a map like this makes me happy.

GREG: Yeah, it's like the process of drawing it makes the place exist.

CHAIRS

It's not just the big picture you have to think about when creating a world. The small details count too. Film-maker Tony Zhou posts fantastic short documentaries under the title *Every Frame a Painting*. He analyses different aspects of film-making: soundtracks, editing, storytelling, directing martial arts, framing comedy. But one of his more esoteric shorts is about the importance of chairs. Chairs can actually say a lot about your characters. Bad guys look good in wingback leather chairs. Slobs look good in threadbare old armchairs. Characters who've lost their love of life look right in functional chairs with grey upholstery. Maniacal kings and queens look good on a throne made of swords. Have a look at two of the characters you've created. What kind of chair would they sit in? Draw their chairs below.

SETTING THE SCENE

Often the beginning of a play, a film or a book will have no characters at all. It will simply introduce us to the world, the landscape, the mood. Look at the start of *Bleak House* by Charles Dickens: 'London ... Implacable November weather. As much mud in the streets as if the waters had but newly retired from the face of the earth,

and it would not be wonderful to meet a Megalosaurus, forty feet long or so, waddling like an elephantine lizard up Holborn Hill. Smoke lowering down from chimney pots, making a soft black drizzle, with flakes of soot in it as big as full-grown snowflakes – gone into mourning, one might imagine, for the death of the sun.'

One of the central themes of the book is the law. The world that Dickens paints reflects the ancient, pondering world of lawyers and barristers and judges. Both the real world and the legal system he ridicules are obscured by thick shadows. Interestingly the book isn't so 'bleak' itself: the wry humour of Dickens, which comes through in this opening passage, infuses the rest of the book too.

In the excellent film *Night on Earth* by Jim Jarmusch, the camera begins in space and flies towards Earth. Then we see a series of clocks (the places we will visit separately in the film). The camera focuses on the clock for Los Angeles. Then we see images – almost like street photography images – a pool, a parked car, a motel, phone boxes, a food van. Once we have a taste for the place and the mood, the fixed camera view finally pans right. We catch sight of a taxi and follow its path down the road. Inside, we meet our first character, played by Winona Ryder.

So let's say Charles Dickens is doing *Bleak House 2: Bleaker Still* and Jim Jarmusch is doing *Night on Earth 2: One More Night*. They are both going to feature your hometown and you want to make your recommendations.

Write an introductory paragraph for Dickens about your town. You may love, or hate, where you live. Let those emotions come through.

Now think of a series of strong images that you could recommend to Jim Jarmusch that would set the scene for where you live. They can be wide shots of key buildings, or closer shots, perhaps of a broken sign or some long-established graffiti.

MONSTERS

Time to look back at those monsters you created earlier in the book. Think about how their personalities might be reflected in their homes. They may live underground, or in a giant clam shell at the bottom of a lagoon, in a nest in a giant tree, or in a two-up, two-down ordinary house. Look at your monsters and draw their homes here. Write down how their personalities are revealed by the world around them.

MONSTER MAP

Now let's draw another map. On this one, you're going to locate your different monsters in different parts of the land. Are there natural barriers to your monsters meeting? Or a no man's land where they share a water hole, or meet for battle?

RANDOMNESS MOMENT!

Imagine three insects in sports gear. Draw them. Invent a sport that they love to play. What is it? And what are the rules?

WORLDS OF WONDER

Think about the places you feel are the most awe-inspiring on Earth. What are they? Why do you love them? Maybe it's a big city or somewhere in the Southern Alps, a great desert or even a part of Antarctica.

Draw a part of this world here. Can you set a story or a character in this world – someone or something that is relevant to this place? Remember, if you're going to be creating a universe, you may as well find the place interesting. You're going to be spending a lot of your time there.

ARCHITECTURE

Does the world you're creating have buildings? If so, what are
they like? Perhaps they are familiar to our world? Houses from
nineteenth-century Paris? Are the buildings piled on top of each
other like a Brazilian favela? Or is the architecture something
new? Like machines that have become buildings. Or buildings made
from the remains of some giant creature. Grab a newspaper or a
magazine. Get your scissors out and start chopping out pictures and
photos. Glue them below to create a row of buildings. You don't have
to use pictures of real buildings if you don't want to. Anything could
be a building: a shell, a watch face, a box, a book.

TOWN PLANNING

MYLES: Remember that I said we wrote a half-hour pilot for an animated sitcom called *Isle of Spagg*?

GREG: It was about a seaside community where a whole bunch of humans, folkloric creatures and mythical beings went about their everyday lives.

MYLES: It was set on an island with one main town, also called Spagg.

GREG: But where did everyone live? Which was the posh part of town? Which bit was the seedy underbelly? Where were the shops? Was there a closed harbour? These were questions we needed to answer before we launched into animation.

MYLES: So we drew a map of the town.

GREG: Well, I did.

MYLES: Yeah, but I pointed at it sometimes and said, 'Maybe this is where Fred lives?'

GREG: Mmm, yeah. Very creative.

Why don't you draw a town map across these two pages?
Give it a name. Point out places of interest.

COFFEE STAIN

Time for goofy. Make yourself a coffee. Make sure you spill a bit so the bottom gets all wet. Now put your mug on this page and make a stain! When it's dry, turn the stain into something – a person, an island, a wheel ... anything you fancy.

NOSY PARKER

Go on to an estate agency website and have a look inside some of the houses. What can you see in the rooms of these strangers? What does it tell you about the inhabitants? Write or draw your thoughts here.

OBJECTIFICATION

Look around you. What objects do you see? Pick one. Imagine you are that object. Now, tell us a story from the point of view of that object.

_____

_____

_____

_____

_____

_____

_____

_____

_____

_____

_____

_____

_____

_____

_____

_____

In my early days I was a lot sharper

MUSIC

If you're trying to capture the mood of a world that you are creating, think about this question: what kind of music exists in your created world? Is there music at all? Is it like something that you already know? Jazz? Ambient? Rock? Or is it something new? Something like the clicking of small pebbles combined with the booms of the sea? What captures the right feel for you? Imagine you're creating a world for extremely small people like the Borrowers. They live in the trunk of a merchant who travels the Silk Road. Or perhaps they live underwater like tiny mermen and mermaids. Or they live on a blue asteroid orbiting a distant red star. What kind of music might be part of their world?

HEY DROOGS!

Characters in a story will hopefully have distinctive ways of speaking. They might be nervous, or forceful. They might speak in short, efficient sentences, or they might ramble. But is there something beyond the personal that marks out their speech as interesting? Is there a way of talking in this world that everyone shares? Period dramas often modify everybody's speech so that it sounds old-fashioned in some way. Fantasy and sci-fi stories sometimes have aliens with whole other languages. Dystopian stories can use their own special lexicon. George Orwell's *1984* had newspeak, a kind of state-sanctioned language constructed to help them control the population's thoughts and expectations. Another interesting example is Anthony Burgess' *A Clockwork Orange*. He created Nadsat, a kind of Russian-English fusion that main character Alex and his friends used. It reminds us of the ways teenagers repurpose language. When we were growing up, everything good was 'wicked' or 'bad'. For the next generation, everything good was 'sick'. The problem with using real words like this is that they date your work. This is perhaps why Burgess created his own, unique version.

Here are a few Nadsat words. Check out the Russian translations against Nadsat and you'll see how close they are.

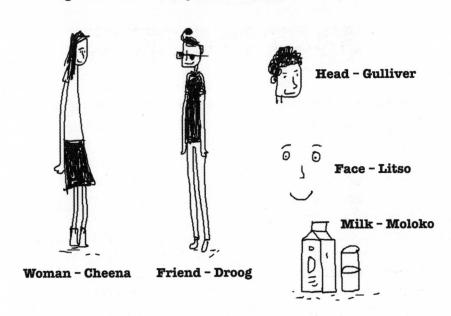

Head – Gulliver

Face – Litso

Milk – Moloko

Woman – Cheena   Friend – Droog

Why don't you create your own words for some key concepts.

To go	-	_____
Friend	-	_____
Enemy	-	_____
Food	-	_____
Thanks	-	_____
Good	-	_____
Bad	-	_____

Of course, the speech of the world you are creating should serve a function, not just be a gimmick. How would people in a militarized universe speak? Or people living semi-wild with animals?

SEE AGAIN

Walk around your home city, town or village. But today try to notice things you've never seen before. Perhaps it will be a swirl on a lamp post. Or a window boarded up with silvered paper. Perhaps you'll notice a person in a window looking down at the street – someone who is used to going unnoticed. What do these places and settings suggest to you? How do they make you feel? Why haven't you seen them before?

_____

_____

_____

_____

_____

_____

_____

_____

_____

_____

_____

As children we are very aware of the world around us because it's so new. We are gathering information about the world and are open to the sights, sounds, smells and touch of things. We might lie on our backs in a summery garden and watch clouds sliding across the blue heavens. But as we grow up our brain fills up with information and at some point it sees a cloud in the sky and just says, 'Yeah, whatever. Cloud. White. Sky. Got that information already.' We start to unsee, unhear and unfeel things. We tune out the stimuli until eventually it's like we're walking around in a giant blankness, a nothing. It's important to tune back in and reconnect with our senses. Apart from anything else it can be a rewarding, sensory experience. But from a creative point of view it can also open up doors in your mind, leading to new insights, or back into old memories. Many of these thoughts and feelings will be ones that seem private, but are shared by many of us. While you're reconnecting with your senses, you'll also be preparing to connect with your audience.

FIVE SENSES

You have five senses. But how often do you focus on each one separately? Stand in a place and think about each sense, one at a time. What are you sensing? What do you see? What can you notice that you didn't see straight away? What can you hear? Take a big breath. What do you smell? Is there something to taste? Reach out and touch something or feel the air on your skin.

NIHILISM

Sometimes you might not want a world at all. When we created our little ninja animations *Fuggy Fuggy*, we wanted to focus on the character's pratfalls, so we made the background as simple as possible using a piece of Japanese textured paper. We only included props that were useful to the comedy in the scene. Everything else was left blank. We've done something similar in our *Turkey vs Pilgrim* Disney shorts where there's a lot of white or blank space. This helps the viewer focus on the comedy action.

Now, look at the space on this page. Prepare yourself.

Now ... don't fill it in.

Don't draw on it.

Or write on it.

Contemplate the emptiness.

MYLES: There's nothing to see here. Move along.

CLOTHES

Actors know how important the right clothes or costumes are
to creating a character. It can make things a lot easier if their
outward appearance is already telling a story. But clothes aren't
just about the characters of individuals; clothes are also a part of
the world. What clothes will you put in your new worlds? Existing
clothes? Contemporary high fashion? An historical costume,
perhaps redesigned for a futuristic purpose? Will it be a mishmash
of different styles, or will everyone wear very similar uniforms?
Clothing says a lot about a person, but also a lot about a society.
Design your own military uniform on a character, then explain
what all the parts of the uniform mean.

FORGOTTEN PLACES

Walk around a town or city nearby. Look for all the places that
have fallen into disrepair. Sketch them, or photograph them, then
get some cheap prints and stick the pictures here. You're looking
for the places that are ruined, or unloved, or battered. Study them.
Who might live here? What kind of a world do they belong
in, if not ours? What stories do they have to tell?
Scribble down your ideas beside the pictures.

INVISIBUILDING

MYLES: I was once walking down Park Street in Bristol when I came across a doorbell. There's nothing strange about this in itself, except that it was not next to a door. Nowhere near one. Or a window. Or anything. Just a doorbell on a large stone wall. Possibly it was some kind of prank, but I prefer to imagine it was some kind of secret doorbell that, had I rang it, might have led to an extraordinary adventure.

GREG: So why didn't you ring it?

MYLES: Maybe I did. Maybe I was replaced by a Myles-shaped demon?

GREG: Erm ... were you?

MYLES: Of course not.

Anyway ... it's fun to imagine extraordinary places are all around us, hidden from view. Think of 12 Grimmauld Place in the Harry Potter stories. The house is invisible to the local 'muggles' (non-magical people). They think the reason there is no number 12 is because of a numbering error. In fact, it's the ancestral home of the Black family, a clan of powerful witches and wizards.

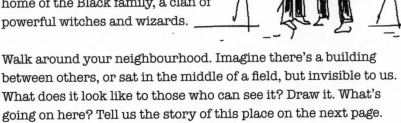

Walk around your neighbourhood. Imagine there's a building between others, or sat in the middle of a field, but invisible to us. What does it look like to those who can see it? Draw it. What's going on here? Tell us the story of this place on the next page.

BEHOLD!

'And God saw everything that he had made and, behold, it was very good.'

Have a quick look back through this chapter at all the things you've created. It's like you've opened little doors from our world into lots of other worlds. At the moment, you can glimpse parts of these other places that you've imagined. The more time you spend looking at them, the more you'll create and the more detail you'll fill in. Perhaps you'll want to create many different places, or perhaps you'll fall in love with one and want to discover more and more about it. Terry Pratchett's Discworld is an amazing universe. He examined it through the lives of many different characters, and in different periods of that world's history. The combined effort of all those stories has gone towards making an extraordinarily complex, funny, familiar yet surprising universe that is loved by millions of his readers.

MYLES: So you have some characters.

GREG: And you've created some worlds.

MYLES: Time to tell some stories!

Here Endeth The Chapter!

PART FIVE
***
STORIES

There are about three billion books on how to write stories and story structure.

We'll mention some of the basics here but ... what we're aiming for in this chapter is something else.

What we have here is a big soup of hints and tips – some of them more useful for making films or animations, some of them more useful for writing books, short stories or graphic novels.

If you want to learn more about the mechanics behind it, then we recommend John Yorke's book *Into the Woods*.

We want to get some ideas flowing, and suggest a few ways of wrangling those ideas into shape. This chapter is all about loosening up and letting the ideas come out to play.

When it comes to structure, there's a spectrum of chaos and order, as we'll find out over the next few pages.

ATMOSPHERE

Before we launch into structure, let's think about some other things that affect how we feel when we hear or see a story played out.

What about mood? How do you want your audience to feel when they are reading or watching what you've created? How can you find ways to communicate the mood?

In graphic novels, the colours, choice of framing and composition of a whole page can make a big impact.

In films and TV, music can do a lot. But so can the point of view of your story. Are you telling it from one person's point of view or from several people's? How can you switch between them to create the most interesting story?

What about the pace and rhythm of your story? Does it have the same pace all the way through? Think about your favourite stories. There are gentle, comforting moments. There are fast and dangerous moments. A story with one rhythm all the way through will bore its audience, and will probably bore you when you're creating it.

Think about how you might change the dynamic of your storytelling to help you create the right atmosphere.

Pick a short song that you like that has a lot of variation in the pace and rhythm. Now listen to it a few times. Start to think of a simple story. Something like:
• a footballer is running up a pitch trying to score a goal
• an astronaut is jetting through the cosmos trying to find his fleet
• a sapling is growing, and trying to break through to become a tall tree
Imagine that the music is controlling the mood of the story at any given moment. What is happening at each moment? **Write or draw your ideas here:**

NO STRUCTURE

GREG: Okay! Back to structure. Or, in this case, no structure!

MYLES: Some people reject the idea of structure in a story. You can deliberately create something with no structure: something without any plan, following a stream of consciousness. Working on these kinds of projects can be very liberating because you just create without any pressure to conform to classical structure. The final product may not make much sense to anyone else, but if it has a mood and an atmosphere, then this may be enough to make an impact.

We created an animation a few years ago called *Codswallop*. It had very little formal structure.

GREG: It began when I started drawing random cartoons on postcards and then posting them back home, addressed to my son. When they arrived back home the postcards went on the wall next to each other. I realized after a while that together they looked like a storyboard. But it was a storyboard made up of unrelated moments. This was the basis for the film. The film has no real narrative, but it does convey a sense of absurdity and a darkening mood that turns more positive at the end.

Why not buy yourself some blank postcards? Draw on one a week and post it back to yourself. Put them on the wall. See what strange and random story builds up over time. (Make sure every drawing is different and unrelated to the previous ones, though.)

A more recent film we made was *365*. This had a very simple structure, explained in the logline for the film: One Year, One Film, One Second a Day. Each day of the year we created one second of animation. There was no prepared storyline, script or storyboard.

The ideas came from things read, seen or experienced on the day, with a little artistic licence for good measure. When put together the film had 365 moments, all one second long. Although there is no narrative, there is a kind of unifying structure that comes from the length of each moment and the fact the whole work represents one year of experiences.

Why don't you set yourself this task: draw or describe every day of the year in one picture, one word or one sentence. Start today!

You can watch both *Codswallop* and *365* online on our Vimeo site.

INTERCHANGEABLE SEGMENTS

MYLES: The next stage in order vs chaos is a story with interchangeable segments. Ever watched a Road Runner cartoon? There's usually a brief set-up. Wile E. Coyote is hungry and wants to eat the Road Runner. Then there are a series of gags and set pieces where the Coyote tries to catch his prey, but comically fails. Finally there's a moment where he either gives up or things go even more catastrophically wrong than usual. This kind of structure is essentially **Beginning**, **Middle**, **End**.

But what's interesting is those middle bits. In most cases you can rearrange them – the gags, the set pieces – IN ANY ORDER. One doesn't lead to another. Each one is just another attempt to kill the Road Runner. Is this a problem? Of course not, because we are laughing and that is the purpose of the cartoon.

Think back to those monsters you created. Imagine one is chasing the other hoping for a tasty monster meal. How many funny scenarios can you think of where the one tries, but fails, to capture the other? **Draw an idea here.**

But most stories don't play this way ...

BUT, THEREFORE

The creators of *South Park*, Trey Parker and Matt Stone, shared a very simple bit of advice about how they construct stories in an MTVU appearance. They said that between each beat of your story there should be the word 'but' or 'therefore'. This way, each moment is affecting the next moment in the story in some way.

The ostrich hid her egg, THEREFORE the lion couldn't find it, BUT then she forgot where it was, THEREFORE she recruited the snake to help look for it, BUT then remembered the snake liked eating eggs too.

Try it yourself. Make up a little story using BUT or THEREFORE to see where it leads you.

_____

_____

_____

_____

_____

BETTER **AND** WORSE

This 'therefore and but' idea is similar to the 'better and worse' game. When we were first starting out we went to a workshop at the Animated Exeter festival. The workshop was run by writers Alan Gilbey and David Freedman. One of the fun games they introduced us to was the better and worse game. Pick one of the characters you have created and imagine they have a journey to go on. They set off from their house and then ... things go badly. But then things go well. But then things go badly again. But then ...

You get the idea. You can play this game to help generate some great story reversals.

MYLES: A giant asteroid was heading for Earth, but then things go better because ...

GREG: A spaceship bumped into the asteroid and knocked it off course, but then things got worse because ...

MYLES: The asteroid bumped into the moon and sent the moon hurtling towards the Earth, but then things got better because ...

GREG: Carry on the story, or start your own on the opposite page:

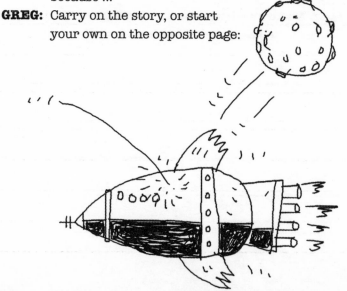

ASKIN' SORKIN

You might have noticed that, with the exception of the most experimental stories, most of these story structures have some basics in common:

- Characters have an intention. They want something

- Characters must face obstacles. These things get in the way of the character reaching their goal

MYLES: Check out Aaron Sorkin's Masterclass online for more on this.

GREG: Oh, is that free?

MYLES: Nope. But it's Aaron Sorkin, creator of *West Wing* and *A Few Good Men*, isn't it!

GREG: Fair enough.

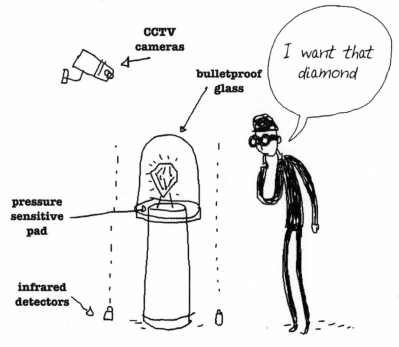

CCTV cameras

bulletproof glass

I want that diamond

pressure sensitive pad

infrared detectors

Now let's say you want to write about a bunch of rabbits who need to find a new place to start a warren. They see a hill far away on the horizon that looks perfect. What are the obstacles they might face on the way? Write them here, or draw a little map of the landscape and point out the problems along the way.

If you're stuck for ideas, watch or read *Watership Down* by Richard Adams to see what he came up with!

159

ACT, ACT, ACT OR ACT, ACT, ACT, ACT, ACT?

If you want to go full-on classical structure, it's time to brush up on act structures. You've probably heard of three-act structure. It's basically beginning, middle and end.

You begin with **Act One**, setting up the world and the characters, then there's a turning point: something big changes. BAM!

We're into **Act Two** where the character's life spins off in a new direction. They go through a lot of development, struggling against obstacles, until they find themselves in a nightmare situation. It's a real test of their character. They make a choice about how to deal with it, and off we go into ...

... **Act Three**, where everything wraps up and sorts itself out.

There are lots of dizzyingly complicated diagrams that explain this. But essentially we are still dealing with the same fundamentals: that characters have an intention and must face obstacles. The acts just give us some idea about the rhythm of the whole story and when they will face the biggest decisions and the most jeopardy.

GREG: If three acts sounds confusing, maybe five acts sounds worse.

MYLES: Actually, it can make things simpler. A lot of storytellers with a new idea have a feeling for how the story starts and how it ends – that's acts one and three sorted!

GREG: But what about that middle bit? You know, the biggest part of the story. How do you structure that?

MYLES: This is where five acts come in handy. Act one stays as act one. Act three becomes act five. Act two is now split into three sections: acts two, three and four. By breaking up this middle part of the story into three parts, it's easier to create some shape.

Here's how it might work:

STORY IN FIVE ACTS
Act one: events are set up ...
Act two: things go well!
Act three: things get tricky
Act four: things become a total nightmare!
Act five: everything is resolved.

You can write a whole film this way. Or just an incredibly short story or poem!

Romeo met Juliet, and Cupid did his thing.
They fell in love and kissed a bit and bought a wedding ring.
But Mercutio, their dying friend, put a curse on both. So,
They hid a bit and tried to trick the world that they were dead.
But a postal perturbation left them really dead instead.

Have a go yourself with these prompts:

Once upon a time . . .

Until a big turning point which was ...

Which led us into act two where, surprisingly, things went well because ...

But then in act three things went badly because ...

And then things became as bad as they could in act four because ...

But then it all resolved in act five because ...

GREG: Okay, did we just grossly simplify act structures?
MYLES: Maybe a bit. But there's a lot of snake-oil salesmen out there when it comes to this stuff. You can really get bewildered about it. You know, they'll say things like, 'Go to the seminar!' 'Buy the T-shirt!' 'Get the book!'
GREG: What, like this book that we're inside right now?
MYLES: No, no. This book's great!

RANDOMNESS MOMENT!

Draw a cyclops, a bi-cyclops and a tri-cyclops. **GO!**

HOW YOU'D WRITE IT?

Here's an interesting exercise. Watch the first few minutes of a TV episode or film. After the first big turning point for the main character, stop the show. Write down what has happened so far. Now, write down how you would finish this episode. What happens next? When you've finished your version, watch the rest of the episode. How similar or different was it? What did you prefer about your version and theirs?

_____

_____

_____

_____

_____

_____

_____

_____

_____

_____

_____

_____

_____

MYLES: I've done this exercise with a few people at children's TV writing workshops. I show them my episode of *Octonauts* (series one, episode nine, 'Remipedes'). This is an eleven-minute episode but I only show it up to 3 minutes 15 seconds and let them work out the rest.

WRITING BY DRAWING

GREG: Sometimes it can help to NOT write when you need to write.

MYLES: What? That doesn't make sense!

GREG: Instead you can draw your way through an idea.

MYLES: Oh. I see. That's clever.

GREG: Maybe a visual gag appears in your head. Draw it! Sketch it!

MYLES: Or you could use storyboards to block out the action.

GREG: Say there's a skydiver. She's about to jump out of the aeroplane.

MYLES: Anything could happen next. It's up to you.

GREG: We're not talking about highly detailed storyboards with accurate perspective here. We're talking about scribbles. Thumbnail scratchings. Speedy sketches. Try filling in the three panels below. Then try telling a different story on the opposite page.

THREE BEGINNINGS

Most stories begin with one of three types of situation.
A loss. Villainy. Or the arrival of something new.

1. A LACK OR LOSS OF SOMETHING

'My diamond has vanished!'

'I have no money to pay.'

'The sun has disappeared!'

'I'm sorry but I've lost my way.'

'If only the Holy Grail had not been lost!'

2. VILLAINY

'If you don't pay me a million
pounds, you can't have your
teddy back.'

**'The police are coming to arrest
you. Honestly they are. But don't
worry, I'll protect you by dressing
you up as a monkey, hiding you
in this circus cage and sending
you to the other side of the planet.'**

'I will free your brother from
prison if you give up being a
nun and become my wife.'

3. A CHANGE IN THE WORLD, OR THE ARRIVAL OF SOMETHING NEW

'I woke up this morning and discovered this new hill. What's all that about?'

'Have you seen what's in the garden? It's a portal to the dungeon dimensions. It's going to play havoc with the petunias.'

'What happened to you, Ionesco?'
'Well, I woke up this morning and I had the head of a rhinoceros.'

'What about you Kafka?' 'Me, well I woke up this morning and I'd turned into a giant beetle.'

MYLES: If you're a bit stuck on where a story begins, imagine it to be one of these three things.

GREG: Something has gone missing, or its whereabouts are a mystery.

MYLES: Or some villain is up to mischief.

GREG: Or perhaps something new has appeared in the world that is going to throw things out of balance.

Let's imagine a story with your monsters, created earlier. Come up with three story ideas. One caused by the loss of something, one due to a deliberate, selfish act, and another because something changes in the world around the monsters. What are your stories?

_____

_____

_____

_____

_____

_____

_____

_____

_____

_____

_____

_____

_____

RAYMOND QUENEAU

I t's not enough to know what your story is about and how it will unfold. You also need to decide on a style. Raymond Queneau took this idea to the extreme by telling the same very short story in ninety-nine different styles. It's a fascinating read. Some versions are extremely short. Some are longer. Some are from a personal point of view, others from the point of view of an onlooker. Some of it is so experimental to be almost (or in fact totally) meaningless. What it lacks in meaning it makes up for in being intriguing, surprising and even amusing.

Here's a simple story.
I was running home, late for dinner, when I noticed an old man in a wide-brimmed hat staring into a pothole in the street. He was whistling a tune, something I think I recognized, although I can't quite place it. I stopped beside him for a moment to look down into the hole but all I could see was darkness. I was going to ask him what he could see, but then I decided against it and raced home. The next day I saw him cycling towards the train station. It was a tandem bike but he was alone.

But what if you told it in note form?
Running home. Late. Old man. Hat. Pothole. Whistling. Familiar. Looked. Nothing. Incommunicado. Home. Next day. Cycling. Same man. Tandem. Alone.

Or in the third person, surveillance style?
Tuesday PM. Subject A (thirties, black suit, mousy hair, spectacles, five feet ten inches, estimate 72 kilos) was rushing along Harrington Street when he made rendezvous with Subject B (seventies, long tan trench coat, wide black hat, six feet, estimate 65 kilos). No words spoken but whistled tune. Perhaps a hidden code? Analysis underway but inconclusive to date. Both subjects

observed pothole for some moments. What did they detect there? Unknown. Are they responsible for said hole? Investigation required. Wednesday AM. Both subjects sighted in close proximity again. One on street. One on tandem bicycle but alone. Potential for dual escape?

Why don't you try retelling this same story but as a fairy tale, or in rhyme, or as a story about superheroes? Have fun!

STORY ENGINES

GREG: So, Myles, you've written a lot of preschool television.

MYLES: Yes, Greg, I have, which is great because I haven't really grown up yet.

GREG: I know. So, tell us, how many episodes do these shows have?

MYLES: Often each series has fifty-two episodes.

GREG: That's a lot of stories!

MYLES: Yes it is, brother of mine. That's why the story engine has to be right.

GREG: A story engine? Is that this sort of thing?

MYLES: Wow! I wish I had one of those.

**A story engine is a story format that allows you to create lots of
different stories in the same universe with the same characters.**

When we were children, there was a charming children's TV show
called *Bagpuss*. He lived in a shop with lots of other second-hand toys
and objects. Every episode would begin when a new object was left in
the shop. They would spend the episode trying to work out what it was,
telling each other stories, singing songs, until they agreed on what it was
and put it away in its rightful place.

In another show, *Mr Benn*, the eponymous character walked into a
costume store and put on a costume, then walked through a magical
door into an adventure relevant to the costume.

In *Star Trek*, the crew of the *Enterprise* are out in the wide expanse of
space. They come across some unknown phenomena and have to work
out what it is before it wreaks havoc on the universe.

These shows all have a story engine
that allows them to tell multiple
stories. For detective shows it's the
different crime and the need to solve
it. For hospital dramas it's the
illnesses and the desire to cure them.

If you want to tell multiple stories,
make sure you know what the story
engine is in your universe.

What are the series you like to read or
watch? What is the story engine that
drives the book or show?

READ BOOKS. YOU CAN'T BE INSPIRED IF YOU HAVEN'T BEEN INSPIRED.

FINISH THIS STORY

The trees talk. Not with mouths or tongues – nothing so obvious. Their language is more subtle. They sing. In trickles of water. In crackles, as sugars travel through membranes of phloem. In haunting shushes of rattling leaves. And trees talk with touch – their roots knot together, tugging and looping, communing under the loam. Often they say nothing to one another, absorbed with their own stretching and blooming and bark-laying. But today they were almost shouting to one another because ...

LISTEN TO YOUR SUBCONSCIOUS

Writer Graham Linehan revealed in an interview with writer and broadcaster Charlie Brooker that he often builds his stories from a single funny image. It will be something almost dreamlike that occurs to him, like one of his main characters walking around an office without a T-shirt on. The image makes him laugh and then he begins to think about what kind of situation could lead to this ridiculous moment taking place in his story.

Imagine you have two or three of these crazy ideas from your subconscious. They could be totally unrelated images. Now set yourself the task of fitting them all into one coherent story. Forcing yourself to find a way to link these events and images in a logical, meaningful way could help you to create a really interesting, unique story.

Find somewhere quiet and sit back and relax. Think about your breathing. Breath in through your nose and out through your mouth. Close your eyes and let your mind wander. What do you see in your mind's eye? Try smashing two unrelated ideas together. Perhaps something that makes you smile or wince. A train with a crocodile on board. A child who believes the ghost of Shakespeare has inhabited her dog.

MYLES: Or something ... ahem ... better!
GREG: Write or draw it here.

GO TO A MUSEUM TO FREAK YOURSELF OUT

MYLES: We live about an hour away from Oxford in England. This famous university town is full of wonderful places to visit, not least the Pitt Rivers Museum. It is stuffed full of fascinating ethnographic and archaeological objects. The museum was founded by General Pitt Rivers in the nineteenth century. We imagine him swanning about the world, like a typical Victorian, saying:

> Oo! That's nice. And it's mine now!

... though we may be doing him a disservice. Anyway, the museum has continued to collect more and more anthropological delights. It's a source of inspiration.

GREG: I've sketched lots of objects here and used some of them in our animation. Do some research about the museums close to you. Is one especially interesting? Go there. Take a sketchbook or a notebook. Spend time studying the exhibits. Perhaps something you see here will inform a character, a world or a story, or all of them.

RE**WRITING**

You've probably heard the phrase writing is rewriting. But what does that actually mean? The last thing you want to do when you've finished the first draft of your story is to think about having to rewrite it.

And that's fine. When you've finished the first draft, slap yourself on your back, say well done and put your work away. Wait a few days. Then come back to it.

Look for the following things in your story. They are good ways to tighten things up.

Have you repeated ideas? Can you cut some text out but keep it clear? Can you enter each scene or chapter later and exit sooner but leave the same story? Are your characters being true to their personalities? Do you have too many characters? What's the minimum number you need to tell the story? Do people need to talk so much? Can things be communicated with the body, or a nod, instead of through dialogue? Do you have whole scenes where nothing much happens? Can you cut them completely? Are you having cars arrive and people walk through doors? Why not start after the car has already arrived, or when the person is already in the room?

It helps to get some feedback from people you trust after your first draft. If something in the story doesn't make sense to them, it's a good sign that you haven't been clear enough in your storytelling.

The director Danny Boyle makes his screenwriters read their scripts out loud to him. It's a good way to understand if your script is working. You can hear any bad dialogue. You can tell where things get too slow or ponderous. You can sense when there's a lack of drive.

FILL IN THE PANELS

Writers should try to write in pictures and illustrators and comic artists should try to write in words. Flexing your brain like this forces you to think about story differently and gives you more tools for creating.

Fill in the missing panels.

LISTEN, READ, WATCH

MYLES: When I was starting out as a writer I would deliberately try to write for different media. My bread and butter came from writing for animation, where there's a big focus on writing good action and visual comedy moments. A lot of the work is non-dialogue or has very little speech. So I decided it would be useful to have a go at writing a radio play. The challenge was to write a story that was communicated without any images, but through sound effects and dialogue alone.

GREG: You may know the exact niche you want to work in, but consider what you might learn from challenging yourself to work in a different medium. Perhaps you're a graphic novelist who's never considered writing poems? Or a screenwriter who knows for a fact you can't draw.

MYLES: Forget these limitations. You don't have to master these other areas, just play around in them like a child in a sandpit to see what you discover. You might find you have new skills to take back to your comfort zone.

GREG: So the comfort zone is located near the sandpit, right?

MYLES: Yes, just behind the area of expertise.

COMPUTER CONSOLE

Draw a computer console here. Fill it with screens, buttons,
levers, dials – anything you fancy.

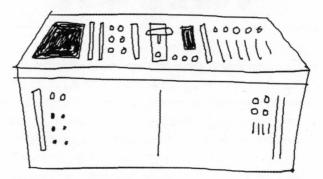

Now tell us what it does. What is the purpose of this machine? What does it measure, or set off, or create, or destroy?

_____

_____

_____

_____

_____

_____

_____

_____

_____

_____

_____

_____

Could this be part of a larger story?

Draw to music

Find some music **you really don't like**. Listen to it. Pay attention
to how it makes you feel. Then begin to draw below.

OFF-SCREEN ACTION

MYLES: One of the things you learn about writing TV for four-year-olds is that you can't have anything going on off-screen. You can't have an important plot point take place without showing it to them. They won't understand what's going on.

GREG: Actually, it's not really that different for adult TV. In the recent hit TV show *Stranger Things*, all of the action occurs to the characters we meet. By that I mean the characters don't spend ages talking about some old uncle who was important in their life, an uncle whom we never meet but who turns out to be important to the story; they talk about each other and do things together, on screen. It's hard to care about someone we haven't met. Even if a character we like cares about this off-screen, non-appearing character, it doesn't mean we will.

MYLES: I was recently writing a script for older kids and had a lot of stuff in my script about my main character missing his mum. The only problem was, we never meet his mum. Thank goodness my script editor Anna Davies pointed this out. We went back and looked at the story and developed a new narrative where my main character had a big bust up with his sister. The main difference was that the sister was an on-screen character. She was 'knowable' to the audience.

PICTURE BIOGRAPHY

Draw a character as a baby or child. Then keep drawing them over and over, at a slightly older age. Perhaps add notes about things that have happened to them, things that might affect the way they look, or might affect their happiness or health. Here's an example.

You might hear people saying things like 'character is more important than plot' or 'plot is more primary that characters'. But really the best stories intertwine what is character and what is story. They become the same thing. We love to hear biographies of the good, the bad and the ugly. Your life is your story, but will also reveal your character.

STORY SLAVES

You may have a very strong idea for your story. But are you making your characters do something out of character to make the story move along?

WELL, STOP IT!

Story should flow out of characters' established personalities. When they start to serve the story like slaves, they lose their authenticity and your whole story will become boring and unbelievable.

If you've created a terrible pirate character who carves up his victims, drinks too much and is violent towards men, women and animals, and then you suddenly make him a bit nicer at the end of your story so that he can help a young girl to find her way home and conveniently wrap up your story ... you will really annoy everyone.

PUSH YOUR CHARACTERS TO THEIR LIMITS BUT KEEP YOUR CHARACTERS CONSISTENT, BELIEVABLE AND LOGICAL

WORDS AND PICTURES

In the media where we combine words
and pictures – graphic novels, TV, games,
films – it's best to avoid moments where
the words and pictures do the same job.

A more sophisticated story shows us one thing, but we hear something
else. It might elaborate on what we see. It might contradict it. On the face
of it, two people shaking hands seems like a straightforward action. But
who knows what's going on behind the scenes?

Draw two friends here. They're meeting for the first time in years. They are delighted to see each other, but instead of saying that, they trade the harshest insults. What do they say to each other?

DEAR DIARY

What other ways can you tell a story? The diary form is a popular way for a story to unfold. This is obviously a specialized form of first-person narrative. The story may appear to be very different in structure to a three-act story but, essentially, you'll still be able to identify a character who wants something, charting the obstacles that get in their way.

MYLES: Here's the beginning of a short story I wrote. It features entries from two diaries charting events that will – at a later point – intersect.

Telescope (a tale of two diaries)

CROBDAY, 35TH OF HANGUST

HA! I, Thorax, the youngest Prince of Noo, am on my way at last.
I have broken through the starwall and am soaring into space. This'll
teach Mummy and Daddy! They may be Intergalactic Empress and Nebula
Overlord of the planet Numnug but they're NOT THE BOSS OF
ME! They have no doubt sent a squadron of Drabian Rescue Ships to
find me. Good luck, morons! Thanks to the invisibility shield around my
rocket they'll never succeed. SO THERE! But I will return. Oh yes. IN
GLORY! Once I have found another planet to vanquish, I will vanquish
it and return as a glorious vanquisher! HA HA!
P.S. Today I learned a new word. 'Vanquish' (verb), meaning to conquer,
to defeat, to overpower.

FRIDAY, 5TH OF AUGUST

Dear diary,
I am bored. I am so bored that I am this bored: bored bored bored
bored bored bored bored. That's really bored. I told Dad. He said, 'Never
mind, Jenna.' I told Mum. She said, 'Why not play with your toys?'
GAH! Have you seen my toys? They're ancient! I'm not a BABY!
I even told baby Tom that I was bored and he said, 'He go ba ge.'
AHHHHHH! Nothing ever happens in the holidays. I'm SOOOOO
BORED!

SLIBDAY, 36TH OF HANGUST

GLORIOUS NEWS. I have searched the cosmos and found my target!
A tiny green and blue planet orbiting a yellow sun. Sensors tell me the
people living there are MEGA-primitive. I will VANQUISH them! Their
puny brains and idiotic machines will be no match for my TUNGERIAN
WAR ROCKET! HA HA! In other news, I received a video message

from Mummy and Daddy (Empress and Overlord) telling me to come home and stop being so silly. They said they were sorry if they'd ignored me, but it was very hard running a solar system. WHATEVER!

SATURDAY, 6TH OF AUGUST

Dear diary,

We went shopping and it was so BORING. Mum refused to take me to the cinema, because she wanted to spend three million years in a shoe shop trying on every single shoe. SHE DIDN'T EVEN BUY ANY OF THEM! AHHHHH! Dad got bored too and went off on his own. I asked if I could come and he said, 'Mumble mumble mumble.' Which is his way of saying NO! Then he came back with a telescope he'd bought and Mum and him had an argument. Mum said Dad had holes in his pockets. Dad said telescopes were useful. Mum said shoes were useful. I said Mum hadn't bought any shoes and she said speech was silver and silence was golden. What does that even mean? AHHH!

Why not try to carry on this story?

_____

_____

_____

_____

_____

_____

DOUBLE DIARY

**Now imagine an important event witnessed by two very
different people. What is it? Think of how their diary entries
leading up to that event would read.**

AUTOWRITING

Are you sat in front of a white page wondering what to write? The answer may be to stop thinking so hard and let your mind just operate by itself. Your brain is capable of almost instantaneous improvization. At any given moment, fourteen billion neurons are firing in your brain. (This is a fact we found on the internet, so it must be true.)

Pick up a book and randomly select a page. Without looking, point your finger at a word on the page. Now look at it. Write the word down, then the two before it, then the two after it. Alternatively, pick out five random words from the same book. These are your prompt words – what you will use to kick-start your imagination to tell a story.

The next step is to start writing and to not stop for five minutes. Don't think about what you are writing. Don't worry about if it's good or not, or even if it makes sense. Just write.

Write whatever comes into your head.

Here's an example that Myles wrote ...

Prompt words: **Ate, young, night-time, recess, pilfer**

The Ate Witches were riding on the Gradons of Smarg when suddenly they saw, far off, the glow in the sky they had been waiting for, for many a long year. A blue glow: more blue and azure than any jewel or gem, or from the core of any blue diamond.

It stirred the heart of Geltra as she
rode her branch through the cold
air. She had waited longer than
the rest and knew that her fate
was entwined with the events
that would now unfold. Without
even looking at one another they
abandoned their mission
and moved as one to the
horizon. The blue glow
grew stronger, though
the night grew darker
and the moon fell from
view.

Finally they reached it and started to
circle lower and lower. There was only ocean
beneath them. And under the deep water a great
light beckoned to them. Fish flapped and fluttered
out of the sea en masse, and prawns and krill
skittered about as though in shallows, despite the
depth of the sea.

Witches from the White Wiccan Farthesters
were also circling, no doubt elsewhere having
seen the same signs from afar. Normally they would

have attacked each other in an instant, but now they circled together, two tribes as one, and came low. Geltra saw Persinog among the White Wiccans and nodded to her. Persinog acknowledged her with a nod back, tacit and stoic, but behind her eyes Geltra thought she detected a kind of warmth, a smile even, which reminded her of the sister she had once been so fond of. It had been too long.

They came low and even as they reached the sea the glowing blue crystal broke the surface, new land, but in the form of a huge copper sulphate crystal – a land made of blue glass. They touched down on it and walked to meet one another. The crystal continued to push up from the sea and after a short while Geltra could clearly see what she had long thought about. Trapped as though in jelly were creatures – butterflies, fish, dogs and, here and there, people. And there, at the heart of the glow, was one person that they all knew – the Rungalot witch of Gruyheg, the source of all their power. The One Witch. The nexus of magic.

MYLES: Apparently I wrote this on 7 July 2011. I found it in my little autowriting folder. The funny thing about autowriting is that you often have no memory of what your wrote afterwards.

GREG: Probably because it comes straight from the subconscious.

MYLES: Reading it back is like reading something written by someone else. Perhaps it will inspire a new idea.

GREG: So what we've learned here is that you have a subconscious fascination for witches, copper sulphate crystals and making up silly names for things.

MYLES: Ringbal the Toofoo of Ninaglog.

Now you have a go ...

THE WORST THING THAT COULD HAPPEN

The most dramatic moment in a story is often when the worst thing that could happen ... does happen. This is the crisis. Our main character has to face the thing they really didn't want to. They have to go through hell. It's the moment the tree of life is cut down, the moment the murderer is found not guilty and set free, the moment the lovers split up.

Try to come up with some worst moments for these scenarios:
A rich man is dying and has a week to live. He decides to leave all of his money to a charity. But ...

_____

_____

A snowman comes to life and decides to explore the world. He befriends a polar bear. But ...

_____

_____

A coffee picker gets a new job in a larger plantation. He falls in love with one of the other coffee pickers. But ...

_____

_____

Knowing what your worst point is can help you to set down some markers for your story. Now you need to work out how things got this bad, and how things play out after this terrible moment.

RANT ALERT!

In the first *Transformers* film (spoilers!) it's revealed that there's this amazing device called the Allspark that can turn machines into a living Transformer. Not surprisingly, the evil Decepticons want to find it so they can make more allies and destroy their enemies, the Autobots. The worst thing that could happen would be for the Allspark to fall into the hands of the baddies. But ... it never happens. Huh? What? The Autobots keep it away from them and then it gets destroyed in a perplexing battle sequence. The result is that the film doesn't seem to have a crisis point or an escalation of the forces of antagonism. How much more heroic would it have been if the baddies did get it and started using it, but then the goodies found a cunning way of getting the upper hand anyway? Plus it's totally unbelievable that Megan Fox would fancy Shia LaBeouf.

ARMAGEDDON!

There's a bomb heading for your town. There's no stopping it. You have time to send one message to one person. Who is it? And what do you want to say? Is there something you've left unsaid that you can reveal now? Write as yourself, or as a character.

WORKING IN PIECES

Sometimes you know parts of your story well. You've imagined them, dreamed them, thought about them on a long drive. But you're perplexed about other parts of the story. Imagine it's a book and you know what's going to happen in Chapters 1, 2, 4, 7, 10 and 15, but you're not sure what's going to happen in the bits in between. That's fine!

Write or sketch down the bits you do know. Enjoy getting them down on paper or typed up. No one says you have to write things from beginning to end. You can write like patchwork until you have a whole piece. Remember, you're just creating a first draft and you can always refine and rework later.

ACTIVE CHARACTERS MAKE AN ACTIVE STORY

Look at your story ideas. Are the characters making things happen or are things just happening to them? If they are simply the victims of circumstance, never affecting the world around them, we may start to lose interest or become frustrated by them. Often characters do resist doing things to start with, desperate to keep the status quo, but then are forced into action by changes in their lives. How can you push your characters to breaking point? You are in charge of this universe and you must be a merciless god.

MYLES: Here's an amazing example I just invented. Your character is an ex-pilot who is terrified of flying. He's taken a domestic flight hoping to win back his girlfriend who is a flight attendant. It's his first flight in years. Then he hears over the intercom that the pilot and the navigator are incapacitated. What will he do?

GREG: Well, that's obvious.

MYLES: Is it?

GREG: Yeah, because that's the plot of *Airplane!*

MYLES: Surely not!

GREG: It is. And stop calling me Shirley.

Can you think of a character with a terrible fear? What is that fear? How can you make them face it? What else drives them, so that they find themselves face-to-face with their fear? What do they do?

_____

_____

_____

_____

SOUNDTRACK

When you're creating something, do you like to have complete silence, or some kind of audio or visual stimuli?

MYLES: Because I write I have to concentrate on what I'm creating. Often I work in silence. Sometimes I even sit with headphones on but without any music because it makes things even quieter. But recently I've also taken to making myself playlists that I can listen to while working on a particular project. I choose music without any lyrics because I don't want to distract the part of my brain that deals with words. So, I've been writing a dystopian drama while listening to Daft Punk, Deaf Center and Marconi Union. The music is dark and pacy and full of suspense. I hope that it helps me write in that way too. But when I write comedy I love to listen to Henry Mancini's soundtrack to the *Pink Panther*. It's such an elegant yet silly suite of songs that it makes me smile inside. Again I hope that translates to the page.

Think of a story you'd like to write or a picture you'd like to paint. What would be on the perfect soundtrack for it?

Create your perfect soundtrack to an indie-style film like _Napoleon Dynamite_ or _Juno_. Or a psychological horror. What are the different moods you are trying to capture? What are the tracks you've chosen?

Film: _____

Tracklist: _____

_____

Film: _____

Tracklist: _____

_____

Film: _____

Tracklist: _____

_____

Film: _____

Tracklist: _____

_____

Film: _____

Tracklist: _____

_____

BUSY BRAIN

Introverts are easily overstimulated. It's why they often like quiet.
Extroverts often find they feel understimulated. They may like
to listen to loud music while working. This is part of the reason
different artists choose to work in different environments. There is
no right or wrong – find the ambience that suits you.

GREG: When I'm drawing there's often a rebellious chunk of
my brain that is sitting there going: HEY, GREG! I'M
BORED! So often I'll just stick on some pulp TV from
Netflix in the background. Suddenly the rebel brain is
happy. He's distracted and I can get on with my work.

MYLES: Greg?

GREG: What?

MYLES: Are you saying you have two brains?

SILENCE

A lot of artists prefer to work in complete silence.

Try it. Find somewhere very quiet.

Resist the urge to listen to music, the radio or to look at your phone. Go back over some of the exercises you've done and try them again, or develop them further.

How does the silence help you?

Are you able to focus and concentrate better?

TELL US A STORY

In this chapter we've looked at a few tips and tricks to get your story brain working. Do you have one idea you really want to work on? Can you sum up your story ideas for it in a sentence or two? These will be your story springboards.

Don't let anyone tell you that your story is the same as something else they've read, watched or seen. Even if your story is about three little pigs and a wolf, you will be able to tell it in your own way, with your own twists and turns and using your own unique voice.

We hope that you now have some characters you love, some ideas for the world they live in, and a few story ideas for them. Next we'll have a quick look at how you can formalize these ideas in one place.

GREG: Tell us a story then.

MYLES: What kind?

GREG: I don't know. Something with jeopardy, drama, death-defying chases.

MYLES: Okay. Well, you know all those monsters we talked about creating?

GREG: Yeah?

MYLES: Well ... RUN!

PART SIX

* * *

A QUICK WORD
ABOUT BIBLES

As we mentioned at the start, a creative bible is a repository of all the thoughts you've created for one particular concept. It's a useful object to refer to if you need to remind yourself about the world you've created. The essentials of it are the things we've looked at here: characters, worlds and stories.

If you are collaborating, it's also useful to make sure everyone working on the same universe is sticking to the same rules. That's why every TV show has a bible. There are lots of different people creating one universe and it needs to be the same one.

But even if it's just you and it's a private project, most of us aren't able to work on something uninterrupted. Life gets in the way!

Having a resource like a bible means you can dive back into your made-up universe and remind yourself of all the amazing ideas you've had. Then you can carry on with the project itself.

So what's in a creative bible?
They usually follow this kind of format:

- A logline. A short pithy sentence that encapsulates the whole idea.
- One-page summary of the idea, featuring the main characters, the nature of the world, the kind of stories we'll be told.
- A breakdown of the major characters, with character descriptions detailing their talents and flaws. Pictures are helpful.

- A description of the most important locations. Once again, pictures are helpful in bringing this to life.
- Story springboards. These are one or two sentences that suggest a whole story. TV series have lots of these because there will be multiple episodes.
- Story outline. There may also be a page or two where one story is written out in much more detail.

In children's TV there's usually a section for curriculum also, as most shows have some kind of learning objective.

Bibles do come in different shapes and sizes, depending on their purpose. A bible aimed at the writers on a show will be great big things filled with all the details they need to know to get the characters right and tell stories that are faithful to the universe that's been created. The same bible will often be dramatically shortened and honed into a few pages for the purposes of selling a show. Buyers don't want to wade through complex backstories about characters. They want to get the idea quickly and be able to make a speedy assessment.

PART SEVEN

***

THE END AT
THE END

PUTTING IT ALL TOGETHER

MYLES: Wow. Part 7!

GREG: Yeah, I know.

MYLES: So now you have a pile of raw material.

GREG: Perhaps you have one idea that's popping out as the one you'd most like to work on.

MYLES: Maybe you have a lead character, a bunch of ideas for a supporting cast, some thoughts on the world they live in and the kind of story or stories you can tell.

GREG: This is great because now when you start making your comic, animation, book or whatever, you'll know loads about it and you'll be less likely to get stuck or run out of momentum.

MYLES: And it'll also help you to keep the whole world you've created alive in the your head at once. You'll be able to think about it as a giant synthesis, and that might lead to even more ideas and possibilities.

GREG: Remember, if you want to share any of your creations on social media, just use the #cyoucreate hashtag. We'd love to see them.

CREATING IS BREATHING

GREG: So you have all this raw material.
MYLES: But it's not the whole picture.

When you actually start to write a story the characters may start
to change or evolve. This is because when you bring them to life
they are no longer static, they are breathing – they are starting
to 'behave'. They are no longer just concepts that you think
might work; they are now characters alive in your story who are
responding to the events around them. It's fine for your characters
to adapt in this way, as long as you are not changing them for the
convenience of your story.

Be prepared for characters you thought were temporary to become
important, and ones you thought would be important to be written
out altogether. It's all good.

FEAR OF BUTTONS

Do you fear the send button? You've typed the email, attached your ideas and now just have to send it off. But that send button ... it's so final, isn't it? Here's some advice:

JUST HIT THE SEND BUTTON!

FEEDBACK

A note on feedback. Getting feedback on your ideas can be very helpful, but you have to choose your moments – and to choose who is best to ask. Stephen King tells us in his excellent book *On Writing* that when he's bashing out his first draft he doesn't share it with anyone. Once he has a whole story, then it's time to get some feedback and constructive criticism. Any earlier and there's a danger of receiving unwanted contributions ... or of hearing feedback that puts you off ever finishing. Have confidence in your ideas and push through when it's painful. You can always fix the weaker parts on the second draft after you've received your useful feedback.

If you are struggling to bring all your ideas together, then consider working with a partner in crime.

We recommend it. Two heads are better than one.

BE AMAZING RIGHT NOW!

MYLES: A quick note on working in the wild world of creativity.
Here's something that's happened to me a few times.

So Myles, here's the basic idea for the show.

It's about a dog, or a cat, and they live with some friends, and one of them is a superhero, but the others don't know it.

I see. That's nice. I like dogs. And cats. Superheroes also.

Great, so pitch me a story.

What? Right now?

Sure!

 When this happened to me the first time, I tried to come up with something.

Er... so there's a dog who can turn into a ... turnip ... and he has to solve a mystery about a stolen cheese ... and er ... that's it! What do you think?

 Beep beep beep

Hello?

 What I've learned to do now is this ...

... because I am not a performing monkey. And neither are you.

I'd love to pitch something, but it will be a lot stronger if I can go away and come up with a really solid idea. I'll type it up and send it over.

Great! Look forward to reading it!

CREATIVE BURNOUT

This book is mainly about getting your ideas flowing. But what if you've had a really busy time working on a project and are feeling overwhelmed? You can feel tired, fed up, uninspired. This is creative burnout. But, come on, is creative burnout a real thing?

I think so!

Me too.

The creative mind is like a muscle. If you do a lot of heavy lifting you need to rest and let it recover. When you're in this state of mind there's a number of things that might happen.

GREG: You might want to stop creating anything at all.
MYLES: Or you might find yourself desperate to work on an idea (or ideas) that is different to the one you are supposed (i.e. being paid) to work on.

The comforting thing to know is that this doesn't last. You will recover. But if you can find a way to have some time out, to rest, to take a holiday ... then do it, and don't put yourself under pressure to be creative twenty-four hours a day, 365 days a year. You're not a machine!

CREATE FOR AN AUDIENCE, BY ALL MEANS.

BUT ALWAYS CREATE SOMETHING MEANINGFUL FOR YOURSELF.

THE END OF THE CHAPTER CALLED THE END AT THE END

It's the end at the end, Greg.

Myles, it's never the end.

You mean there's always the next story or painting or song?

Of course. The end is just the beginning.

Especially if you're trying to string *The Hobbit* out over three films.

Oh yes. Good point. Maybe this should just be the actual end of the end then?

Yes.

THE END!

To be continued!   SHHH!

NOW GO AWAY AND MAKE SOMETHING!